Lionel C. Hopkins

The Origin and Earlier History of the Chinese Coinage

Lionel C. Hopkins

The Origin and Earlier History of the Chinese Coinage

ISBN/EAN: 9783337164164

Printed in Europe, USA, Canada, Australia, Japan

Cover: Foto ©ninafisch / pixelio.de

More available books at **www.hansebooks.com**

ART. IX.—*On the Origin and Earlier History of the Chinese Coinage.* By L. C. HOPKINS, M.R.A.S.

THE origin and earlier history of the Chinese coinage have been discussed in several European works, of which the most important are, in order of date, Dr. W. Vissering's "On Chinese Currency," Leiden, 1877; Professor S. M. Georgievsky's "Drevneishia moneti Kitaichev" (The Ancient Chinese Coins), 1889; and M. Terrien de Lacouperie's "Catalogue of Chinese Coins," printed by order of the Trustees of the British Museum, 1892.

The second of these productions, being in Russian, is to my great regret inaccessible to me. Curiously enough, the other two are both in English, though neither of their authors claims that nationality.

In many ways Vissering's volume is a most meritorious achievement. The scheme of the book is excellent; the author has obviously spared neither time nor labour nor zeal on his task, and wherever he gives a full translation, he adds the Chinese text. Here unfortunately is the weak point of the work. The translations are so very defective as in many places to be useless. I do not know whether I am right in my conjecture, but this part of Vissering's undertaking gives me the impression that his translations of a text which offers numerous difficulties, have been made with the help of dictionaries only, and without the immense, the indispensable advantage of references to and consultations with living native scholars. I do not believe there exists a single Occidental student who has acquired Chinese in China or amongst Chinese, that will dispute the opinion of Dr. Bretschneider, quoted and confirmed by Professor G. Schlegel in the T'oung Pao, vol. i. p. 119, in these words—"The mistakes he [Dr. Hoffmann] made were principally due to the insufficiency of our Chinese dictionaries, and to his never having been in China. We quite agree, in this respect, with Dr. Bretschneider, when he says: 'that *it is impossible to make correct translations* from Chinese *in Europe* [the italics are not mine] without the assistance of a good native scholar; excepting, of course, those sinologues who have studied the language in China, and who have studied it for a long time.'"

Hence every allowance ought to be made for Vissering's shortcomings in this respect, if, as seems to have been the case, he had learnt Chinese in Europe only.

M. Lacouperie has not dealt, I regret to point out, fairly by his predecessor in these numismatic studies. The only reference to Vissering's work that is to be found in the whole of the "Catalogue" is in a single footnote on p. lxviii. of the Introduction, and is to this effect: "It [viz. Ma Tuan-lin's Section on Currency] forms . . . the bulk of Dr. W. Vissering, *On Chinese Currency, Coin and Paper Money*, Leiden, 1877." Yet M. Lacouperie is abundantly indebted to the Dutch author. Over and over again he makes use of Vissering's work, sometimes without alteration, oftener with slight verbal changes, omissions, or additions, frequently with somewhat more material modifications, but always without acknowledgment. Between pages 338 and 431 of the "Catalogue," I have marked no less than forty-four passages thus silently adopted.

With regard to the "Catalogue of Chinese Coins" itself, I wish to be perfectly frank. Having had occasion to examine it closely—and I doubt if any other person has spent so much time over this book as I have—I came to certain conclusions which led to the preparation of the present paper. I found, as I believed, many demonstrable errors, many mere conjectures of the author's stated as though they were well ascertained and acknowledged facts, and a number of difficult points which merited much more thorough investigation than they had yet received. In view, therefore, of the authoritative character of a volume issued by the Trustees of the British Museum, I felt impelled to endeavour to the best of my powers to present the available data of this obscure and intricate subject, as they emerge after what has been, I know, a long and careful, and, I hope, an unbiassed examination of all the materials accessible to me which throw light on the first stages of the Chinese monetary system.

Before plunging into the rather tangled details which it has been necessary to gather together and arrange, it may be as well to indicate concisely what appears to be shown, and what, though not demonstrable, is suggested, by the evidence available for forming conclusions.

The actual origin of the earliest form of their metallic money is clearly unknown to the Chinese. But tradition, already embodied in the work known as Kuan Tzŭ, and afterwards repeated in the Lu Shih of Lo Pi, attributes to the founders of the Hsia and Shang dynasties the casting of metal from mountains which are named into what may have been merely ingots, with the object of relieving distress in times of flood and drought.

But Kuan Tzŭ gives us, and in considerable detail, particulars of the use of " treasure " in the administration of his agrarian polity by a still earlier ruler, the legendary Emperor Shun. Chinese numismatists, relying upon these passages in Kuan Tzŭ, believe that a few of these " treasures " have come down to historical times, and that they are represented by the archaic inscribed pieces of peculiar shape discussed below under the heading of *Pi ch'éng ma*. This attribution is by no means free from doubt, and is partially founded on a reading of the legends on the pieces which is itself most questionable.

It would appear probable that at a later epoch, say about the beginning of the Chou dynasty, two distinct types of metal money, with corresponding names, possibly characterizing different regions or political centres, were already in existence—the knife-money and the wedge-handled *pu*. The former seems to have been mainly current in what is now the province of Shantung. Whether a third type, the circular coin pierced in the centre, may not also have been in use in some parts of the country seems impossible to decide. The History of the Earlier Han dynasty is the ultimate source of our knowledge of the next stage.

According to this work, a Minister, not himself a native of the Chou State, but employed by the founder of that dynasty, instituted (which may mean either invented, or simply introduced), for his master's benefit, a "system of currency." This system included squares of gold of a fixed weight, lengths of silk and hempen cloth of definite dimensions, and, lastly, round copper or bronze coins having a central square hole, which the historian speaks of as *ch'ien*, a name the true origin of which is most obscure, but which remains their designation to this day. It is a matter of question whether the term *ch'ien* was, in the first instance, applied to this round copper coin, or whether it was preceded by the word *ch'üan*, and, if either of these names *was* so applied, whether other terms may not have been employed besides. Further, we do not really know whether these coins were inscribed or not.

The next point is reached in the statement recorded in the same history that a larger coin than was then current was cast by the Chou sovereign Ching, and was inscribed with the words *pao huo*, "valuable exchange." Specimens of archaic appearance are preserved which have this legend on them, as well as others bearing the numbers "four" and "six" before the character for "exchange."

It would be unsafe to infer that there had been no change whatever in the currency of the Chou realm in the interval of nearly six hundred years that had elapsed between the reign of Ching and the establishment of the dynasty. Still less should we be justified in assuming that in the various other States, one uniform and continuous type had prevailed during this considerable period. Probably some of the round coins which have come down to us, and the date and locality of whose issue cannot be certainly determined, may reach as far back. Many of them have round instead of square central holes.

After the consolidation of the Empire under the Ts'in dynasty, the History of the Earlier Han tells us, two forms of money alone were in use—gold, and copper *cash* inscribed *pan liang*, "half ounce"—the other varieties of currency, such as pearls, jade, tortoise-shell, shells, silver, and tin being discarded.

Such is a brief outline of the main facts collected in the entries that follow below, bearing on the origin and the earliest stages of money in the group of States and principalities which have since become the Chinese Empire.

There are two extracts from native works which must be considered somewhat fully, and may conveniently stand here at the head of the separate entries dealing with the numismatic terminology.

The first is a famous passage from the Section on Food and Commerce, of the History of the Earlier Han dynasty. The second is taken from the Section on Money in the great Imperial Encyclopædia, the T'u Shu Chi Ch'êng.

Brief as the Ch'ien Han Shu passage is, and simple as it looks, it contains two or three short clauses which were very perplexing to me at first, but having had the great advantage of consulting both Dr. Legge and Mr. Watters, and quite recently, H. E. Shao, the present Governor of Formosa, I believe the meaning to be substantially as here given. The text runs:—

凡 貨 金 錢 布 帛 之 用 夏 殷 以 前 其 詳 靡 記 云
太 公 爲 周 立 九 府 圜 法 黃 金 方 寸 而 重 一 斤
錢 圜 函 方 輕 重 以 銖 布 帛 廣 二 尺 二 寸 爲 幅
長 四 丈 爲 匹 故 貨 寶 於 金 利 於 刀 流 於 泉 布
於 布 束 於 帛 太 公 退 又 行 之 於 齊

"No particulars are recorded concerning media of exchange, gold and copper money, hempen cloths and silks, before the time of the dynasties of Hsia and Yin. T'ai Kung instituted the currency of the Nine Treasuries, on behalf of the Chou: gold, in pieces of an inch square, weighing one *chin*; copper coins, circular with a central square, their weight reckoned in *shu*; hempen cloths and silks, in breadths of two feet two inches, and in length four *chang* [40 feet of the period]. Hence, with regard to commodities, high value [was reflected] in the gold, utility in the knives, their onward flow in the [copper] currency, their diffusion in the cloths, and their compactness in the silks. After the retirement of T'ai Kung [from Chou] the system was again applied in Ts'i."

The first point to which I would draw attention is that the expression *yüan fa*, which I translate ' currency,' seems, on the face of the text, to be applied to all three varieties mentioned, the gold, the cloths and silks, and the copper coins. But Chinese writers on the subject, so far as I have seen, restrict the term to the last of the three.

It will also be remarked that the passage really consists of a statement of fact, for which the author probably had documentary warrant extant in his time, and of a highly symbolizing gloss or comment on the facts, proceeding from the author, Pan Ku, himself, or some earlier scholar whose view commended itself to him.

Vissering, on p. 8, referring to this passage, which is partially quoted in an extract from Chêng Chia-chi, translates the words *liu yü ch'üan*, etc., " it streams faster than a fountain, spreads more (widely) than cloth-parcels, is more precious than gold, and more advantageous than knives"; and he is followed in this by the late Professor von der Gabelentz in his *Chinesische Grammatik*, p. 292. Beyond all question such an idiom is commonly employed in expressing adjectival comparison, but there can, I think, be little doubt that in this instance such an interpretation cannot be put upon the text.

The remaining passage, which is extracted from the Section on Money in the great Imperial Encyclopædia, is in the nature partly of a paraphrase of, and partly of a gloss upon, the previous extract, and is from the pen, if I mistake not, of the Editors of the Encyclopædia themselves.

" ' The Nine Officers [viz. the chiefs of the Nine Treasuries] controlled the offices for valuables and treasure,' and the objects of their control were of three classes, viz. gold, stuffs of cloth and silk, and copper money (錢 幣, ch'ien pi). The gold pieces were designated by the name Gold [cf. Gulden]; the cloths and silks were measured by the piece; the copper money was weighed by the shu. Accordingly, whenever any commodities were paid in or out, it was by means of the copper currency (yüan fa) that their values were equalised and made convertible (均 而 通 之, chün érh t'ung chih). Thus one catty of gold was equivalent to so many copper cash (錢, ch'ien); one piece of silk was equivalent to so many copper cash, and so on. In this way the Government had a standard of measure. All sorts of commodities reflected their [respective] characters—of high value in the gold pieces, of utility in the knife-coins, the power of circulating in the copper currency, the power of distribution in the cloths, and of accumulation in the silks (一 切 財 貨 寶 之 以 金 利 之 以 刀 流 行 之 以 泉 施 布 之 以 布 收 聚 之 以 帛).

"The term 'gold' indicates the 'square inch weighing one catty' of the [Ch'ien Han Shu] text; the term 'knives' indicates the 'knives forming the lowest class of valuables,' of Kuan Tzŭ; the term ch'üan, 泉, refers to the yüan fa, or copper currency; and the 'stuffs of cloth and silk' refer to those described as 'in length four chang the piece.' "

Here, we may note, the editors regard the terms ch'üan and yüan fa as synonymous.

In the ensuing entries I have purposely inserted the Chinese text of passages translated only where it is really indispensable. The system of transliteration is that of Sir Thomas Wade, from which I have only departed in the cases of one or two dynastic or geographical names, such as Ts'i for Ch'i, and Ts'in for Ch'in, from a desire to follow the more usual spelling of these words, and thus avoid a source of confusion. Words within square brackets are always comment, explanation, or amplification of my own. Thus inserted, they interrupt the reader less, I think, than when subjoined as footnotes.

I wish to express my thanks to the Rev. Dr. Legge for valuable assistance given me on various points in the earlier part of the preparation of this article.

Ch'an pi, 鏟幣 ⎫
Ch'an pu, 鏟布 ⎬ Spade money, or perhaps Plane money,
for the definitions of *ch'an* in the Shuo Wên and Liu Shu Ku point to a plane or chisel rather than a spade.

In M. Lacouperie's Introduction to the "Catalogue," p. xviii., we find the entry, "*Pi tch'an*. Spade money. Name given by numismatists to the copper currency of that shape issued by private people, and afterwards regularly in the seventh century, in imitation of small implements of husbandry, which had been found convenient for barter."

Both Williams and Giles have *pi ch'an* in their dictionaries, but I have, so far, not met the term in any Chinese work.

The Chin Shih So heads its illustrations of these coins with the reversed and more natural form *ch'an pi*.

The Ku Ch'üan Hui classifies these so-called spade coins as *k'ung shou pu*, or hollow-headed *pu*, and says (Section Yüan, ch. 10): "Their shape resembling a *ch'an*, they are popularly called *ch'an pu*, or spade money. The upper piece is hollow. The Chi Chin Lu says, 'the hollow was fitted with a handle to hold them by when in circulation,' and adduces from the Odes the passage '抱 布 貿 絲, to carry *pu* to barter for silk.' [But the accepted interpretation of this passage holds *pu* to be *cloth*, and not the metal money which the Chi Chin Lu sees in the word.] The Huo Pu Wên Tzŭ K'ao says the hollow part was fitted with a vertical slip of bamboo, which was pinned in from the side to prevent it slipping out." Li Tso-hsien, the author of the Ku Ch'üan Hui, concurs in all the above, and adds that this type of *pu*, being mostly dug up in Chung Chou, the modern Honan province, dates probably from the Liu-Sung, or Wei dynasties [fifth and sixth

centuries A.D.], though some specimens must, he thinks,
be earlier.

M. Lacouperie regards the *pu* money, in the restricted
sense in which he uses that term, as degenerate forms of
the Spade money, but such evidence as there is affords no
support to this view.

Ch'êng ma huo, 乘 馬 貨 ⎱
Ch'êng ma pi, 乘 馬 幣 ⎰ See *Pi ch'êng ma.*

Ch'i tao, 契 刀 . A graving knife, or knife for carving
wood. The name of a coin shaped like the combination
of a *cash* and a knife blade, issued by Wang Mang.

Vissering, followed by M. Lacouperie, has misunderstood
the meaning of *ch'i tao,* which the former translates (p. 50)
"Knives to make agreements or bonds," and the latter
by "Bond-knife" (Intr. p. xvii.) and "Binding-knife"
(p. 312). Neither writer remembers to enlighten us as to
what meaning they attribute to these expressions.

In the Ch'ien Han Shu the form of the character *ch'i*
used has the radical *ta, great,* but the author of the
Ku Ch'üan Hui, supported by the extant specimens of
the coin, maintains that this form is wrong, and that the
character should have been written with the radical *mu,
wood.* The word signifies to *carve,* being synonymous with,
and in Kanghsi defined by, 刻, *k'ê, to carve.* The Liu
Shu Ku states that *k'ê* implies deeper carving than *ch'i.*
According to the Ku Ch'üan Hui, Wang Mang, who
affected antiquarian tastes, reproduced in these coins an
ancient variety of knife.

Chia ch'ien. See under *Yü chia ch'ien.*

Chien chin, 兼 金 . Double gold.

Couvreur in his dictionary, quoting this expression from
Mencius, defines it as "or très fin qui valait deux fois l'or
ordinaire." But M. Lacouperie, p. xix., asserts that the
first word "must be read 鎌, *sickle,* appropriate name of the
curved knife-shape of the currency of Ts'i." As, however,
the above character for *sickle* is read *lien,* and never *kien* (or
chien), M. Lacouperie, to be consistent, should transliterate
the phrase *lien-kin* instead of *kien kin* as he does.

The knives of Ts'i are, moreover, quite unlike a Chinese or any other sickle. The whole statement is a mere guess which will not bear examination.

Ch'ien, 錢. Copper money.

Considerable obscurity surrounds the origin of the word *ch'ien*, an obscurity that affects both the date of its introduction and the history of its meaning.

In the first place the syllable has another, probably earlier, and possibly unrelated meaning. Thus in the Odes the character occurs once, with the sound *tsien*, in the " rising tone," and standing for the name of some field implement usually translated " hoe." So again we find in the Shuo Wên, under this character, this entry : " A hoe (銚). In ancient times a field implement. From 金, *chin*, *metal*, and 戔, *chien*, giving the sound. The Odes have, ' prepare your hoes (錢) and mattocks.' One authority says, ' valuables ' [一 曰 貨 也]." Tuan Yü-ts'ai, commenting on the above passage of the Shuo Wên, observes that the Elder Hsü's edition does not contain these last four words.

Under the character 貝, *pei, a shell*, the Shuo Wên is rather more communicative, for we there read, " In ancient times they exchanged shells and prized tortoise-shell. Under the Chou they had money (泉, *ch'üan*). By the time of the Ts'in, shells went out of use, and *ch'ien* were current." Tuan Yü-ts'ai notes a suggestion that the reading here should be 泉, *ch'üan*, not 錢, *ch'ien*.

The Shuo Wên's recognition of *ch'ien* in the sense of money may not be free from doubt, but that the word had been so used in literature before the date of its publication is certain. It is frequent in the work known as Kuan Tzŭ. The Kuo Yü also contains it (as M. Lacouperie points out), and a commentator on the Chou Li affirms that the name Ch'üan Fu, or Treasury of Money, mentioned in that work, was sometimes written Ch'ien Fu. With that possible exception, the character does not seem to be met with in the Chou Li.

But there is a consensus of opinion among native

scholars that *ch'ien*, as a term for money, was preceded by an earlier word, or, as some of them think, by an earlier form of the same word. This prior form is now written 泉 and pronounced *ch'üan*, and is fully treated below in a separate entry.

Li Tso-hsien, the author of the Ku Ch'üan Hui, cites the T'ung Chih (I presume Chêng Ch'iao's work of that name) as asserting that under the Emperor Yao money was called *ch'üan*, while the term *ch'ien* did not come into use until the introduction of the "coinage of the Nine Treasuries" at the beginning of the Chou dynasty, or, as he considers the Kuo Yü to imply, until much later, under the Emperor Ching, the 24th sovereign of that dynasty. "There are," adds Li, "slight discrepancies in these accounts, but, summing up the evidence, we see that *ch'üan* was the earlier and *ch'ien* the later term, and that while *ch'üan* includes *ch'ien*, the latter does not include *ch'üan*."

Tuan Yü-ts'ai, in his notes on the Shuo Wên under the word 貝, *pei*, after quoting a statement of Chêng Ssŭ-nung that "in old books *ch'üan* is occasionally found written *ch'ien*," observes that Chou dynasty authors sometimes used 'borrowed characters,' as in this case, and that the writers of the Ts'in dynasty treated the borrowed character *ch'ien* as the correct form. "Hence," he concludes, "it is clear that what the Ts'in and the Han called *ch'ien*, the Chou called *ch'üan*," adding that we have here an instance of what Chinese philologists designate 古 今 字, *ku chin tzŭ*, literally "ancient and modern characters," that is, the same word written under an earlier and a later form. So, too, a commentator on the Kuo Yü is quoted by the Editors of the T'u Shu Chi Ch'êng, in the Section on Money, who says, "anciently they spoke of *ch'üan*, which was afterwards modified into *ch'ien*."

The question then arises, What was the cause and explanation of this substitution of *ch'ien* for *ch'üan*? The data at present seem too few to permit more than conjecture on the point. Perhaps in this substitution we should see the introduction of a new and entirely unrelated term, though why, if so, the new term for circular money should be one that properly denoted a hoe or some such implement is not evident. But this clearly was not the opinion of Tuan Yü-ts'ai and others. Tuan seems to imply some gradual change, apparently, of pronunciation, such that the borrowed character 錢 answered better to the altered pronunciation of the word for money than did the former and proper character 泉. This again implies that only part of the senses of this word *ch'üan* had changed in sound, viz. the sense of *money*, for had all changed uniformly, there would have been no discrepancy felt and no new character needed. This variety in pronunciation would be compatible with the retention of the old sound for the probably original sense of *water-spring*, and the evolution of a modified sound for the secondary meaning of *money*.

There is still a third possible explanation. At the time when, and in the region where, *ch'ien* first came to be used instead of *ch'üan*, the two characters may have had the same sound, and confusion may thus have arisen. In favour of this hypothesis the character 線, *hsien*, *thread*, may be brought forward. In all the accessible dialects the word itself agrees closely in sound (apart from tone and what is technically called ' series,' which affects the quality of the initial) with the sound of *ch'ien*. And the character is composed of *silk* + a phonetic which is now 泉, *ch'üan*, but was once 戔, *or the same phonetic as* that of *ch'ien*. Hence we should infer that 泉 and 戔, and therefore 錢, were once homophones, for the initial is really the same in all.

On the other side, it may be urged that though in the modern Chinese dialects there is no great dissimilarity between the sounds of the two words 錢, *ch'ien*, and 泉, *ch'üan*, and in some the approximation is very close, in the Japanese form alone is there an identical pronunciation —*sen*—for both characters. But if the modern dialects do not support this last-mentioned hypothesis, neither do they afford convincing evidence in disproof, and with this negative conclusion I will leave that part of the question.

Tai T'ung, the author of the Liu Shu Ku, has an interesting passage under the word *ch'ien*, in which he gives his views as to the rise of metal money. He defines the word as "Money, 泉 布, *ch'üan pu*. In ancient times," he goes on, "they carried on trade merely by using what they possessed in exchange for what they did not possess. Owing to the impossibility of an exact equivalence in value between commodities, the numberless differences in price could not be equalized. Accordingly, cloth and silk were made into currency, 幣, *pi*. Such was the origin of currency. Owing to differences of length, breadth, and texture in cloths and silks, fabrications sprang up. Hence came the use of metal knives and tortoise-shell as media of exchange, and the supply of these having been exhausted, there arose *ch'ien* or metal money. Thereafter commerce throughout the Empire was first made uniform. T'ai Kung established the Coinage of the Nine Treasuries, where he cast metal money, *ch'ien*, round externally and square internally (外 圓 內 方), its weight being reckoned in *shu*. From that time onward successive ages valued it as the medium of exchange. The author Po [伯 氏 = ?] writes: 'the designation *ch'ien* was the abdication of the terms *ch'üan* and *yüan* (圓).'"

What, finally, was the origin of the *cash*, this round coin with its distinctive square central hole, and what suggested such a type?

M. Lacouperie's answer appears simple enough if we take only what he says on p. 319 of the "Catalogue" under the heading of "Round Money," for he there derives this Round Money—the *cash* of common parlance—from an alleged Ring Money of the Chou dynasty referred to in the Shu King. But this explanation is complicated by the statement made on p. xviii. of the Introduction, under entry 24, which runs as follows: "錢 *Tsien*, hoe money. *Tsien* was formerly a light instrument of husbandry, perhaps a hoe or sickle, although it is applied at present to the mattock." [This is an error: *ch'ien* as a name for any field implement is unknown in modern Chinese. M. Lacouperie has misunderstood the passage of Williams to which he refers.] "When currency in the shape of various implements of the kind was an historical fact, the term was used as a general designation . . . ."

It does, I confess, seem to deserve more explanation than M. Lacouperie gives it that a word meaning *hoe* should have come to be specially attached to a round coin in every way unlike a hoe, and, as he contends, not derived by modification of its shape from the latter, but from a ring. However, as will be seen under Huan, 鍰, there is no evidence that the latter was a ring. Even had it been so, a mere ring has too vague a likeness to the *cash* type to make the identification convincing.

Another opinion is that the *cash* represents the round and pierced end of the handle of the old knife-coins, of which it should be considered a sort of degenerate survival, and certain knife-coins of Wang Mang the Usurper, for instance those figured in the "Catalogue" on pp. 311–318, are pointed to as exhibiting an intermediate stage. Against this must be set the plain and unmistakable statement of the History of the Earlier Han dynasty, already cited, that coins essentially similar to the modern *cash* were cast as far back as the beginning of the Chou dynasty. This appears almost conclusive against the degeneration theory.

I venture to suggest a different origin which had occurred to me before I found it expressly asserted in Kanghsi's Dictionary under the word 錢, *ch'ien*. It is that the *cash* is a mere reproduction in metal of the 璧, *pi*, or jade-stone token, which with the 圭, *kuei*, resembling it in material and function though not in form, was variously used under the Chou dynasty as a badge of rank, a proof of diplomatic authority, and a sacrificial symbol. It will be seen below that the same symbolical character is attributed to the *pi* as to the *cash*, and, what is noteworthy, the same peculiar terms are used to describe the parts of each. "In the course of time," we read in Kanghsi, "changes were made.

The Emperor Ching cast large coins called *pao huo*. The field and the central hole had raised rims . . the coins were in shape like 璧, *pi*, and so the terms *field* (肉, *jou*) and *hole* (好, *hao*) were also applied to them."

We may devote in conclusion a few lines to the *pi*, or jade-stone token.

The Shuo Wên defines the word as a "token of jade round in shape." The Liu Shu Ku writes thus: "A circular token of jade, rounded externally and having a central hole. Its substance is termed its flesh, 肉, *jou*; the hole is called *hao*, 好." From the Shuo Wên's definitions of the two characters that follow *pi* in that work, and from the Erh Ya, we also learn that when the field was double the hole, the token was called a *pi*; when the field and the hole were equal [in breadth], the name was *huan*, 環; and when the hole was double the field, the token was styled a *yüan*, 瑗.

Ch'ien fan, 錢范. A mould for making coins.

Ch'ih tsê ch'ien, 赤仄錢. Red and sloping money, or, possibly, red-edged money.

This is a name given to certain 5-*shu* pieces coined apparently in the second year of the Yüan Ting period of the Han Emperor Wu, answering to the year B.C. 115. The name was given, according to one view, because of a raised rim of red copper added to prevent the filing away of the body of the coin.[1] But this is not accepted by others. The Ku Ch'üan Hui devotes a page to the point:—

"The P'ing Chun Section of the Shih Chi, or Historical Records, states that the Emperor Wu directed the coinage authorities of the Capital to cast *ch'ih tsê cash*. The commentator Ju Shun observes that the raised rim was of red copper. We are ignorant," adds the author of the. Ku Ch'üan Hui, "of the method of casting employed, but I think that the *pan liang* coins [which preceded the 5-*shu* pieces] were not filed after casting, whereas the 5-*shu*

---

[1] Another popular and apparently similar name is given in the Chin Shih So, viz. 字紺錢, *tzŭ kan ch'ien*, the exact meaning of which I cannot ascertain.

coins were subjected to filing by the people for the sake of the copper dust, and a raised rim was accordingly added. But they continued to be filed down. As a result of filing, the colour of the rim looked new and therefore red, hence the name 'red-edged,' but there was no distinct type of coin made with that name." A certain Liu Ch'ing-yüan is also quoted to the effect that in Shensi he had seen 5-*shu* coins which were thin on the side where the character "5" was, and thicker on that where "*shu*" stood, so that when three of them were put one on the top of another, they looked like a horse's hoof. This presumably means that when the thicker part of each rested on the corresponding part of the one below, the outline of the three together resembled a horse's hoof seen in profile. Liu points out that in the Ch'ien Han Shu, *tsê* is written 仄, which is defined by the Shuo Wên as meaning "inclining, sloping" (側 傾); the expression 赤 仄, *ch'ih tsê*, then, would mean *red and sloping*, but the former word applies not to the rim only. Li Tso-hsien thinks this view is worth consideration.

Vissering has fallen into a most elementary blunder in transliterating these two characters as *Yik-tseu* (p. 43). What his mistake has been caused by is clear enough, though it is singular that such a slip should have escaped him in reading the proofs. He has printed 赤 and translated "red" correctly, but has transliterated the word as *yik* as though the character were 亦, "*also*," which differs, as will be seen, by one stroke.

But if Vissering's blunder be strange, what shall we say when M. Lacouperie follows his predecessor into the same pitfall, and this not merely once, but several times, as on pp. xix. and xxx. of the Introduction, and on p. 360, though he is right on p. 326? There was only one thing left to do to complete the confusion, and M. Lacouperie has done it. On p. 404 he writes: "It was in the first year *Tch'ih-wu*, 亦 烏 [*sic*], *i.e.* 328." The first year of *Ch'ih-wu* was A.D. 328, but the characters as printed in the "Catalogue" are *i niao*!

Chin, 金. Besides its ordinary meaning of *metal* and *gold* (the latter by abbreviation for 黃 金, *huang chin*, "*yellow metal*"), this word has had also a technical sense denoting a special monetary unit, which has varied at different periods.

A writer quoted in the Jih Chih Lu (ch. xi., art. 黃 金) as Ch'ên Tsan, who is perhaps Hsieh Tsan, 薛 瓚, states that under the Ts'in dynasty one *yi*, 鎰, made a *chin*, while under the Han one *catty* made a *chin*, the value of the *chin* thus being considerably less under the later than under the earlier line, for the *catty* was and is 16 *liang* or ounces, while the *yi* has been variously equated with 20, 24, or 30 ounces.

Yen Shih-Ku in his edition of the History of the Earlier Han has a note on the words of the text which speak of the Han using 黃 金 一 斤, "one *catty* of gold," to the effect that this was a reversion to the Chou system, but with a substitution of 斤, *chin*, a *catty*, for the latter's 金, *chin*, a *gold piece*.

Nor, apparently, was it under the Chou dynasty that this gold *chin* unit was first known. For we find in the chapter on Yu Yü Shih, or the Emperor Shun, in the Lu Shih, a passage telling us that the money or metal pieces made by that shadowy ruler was of one *chin*, 金, two *chin*, two *chin* four, and two *chin* five (what the fractional parts may have stood for is not clear), and the same authority adds that the two *chin* five pieces were the heaviest, and the one *chin* the lightest.

And this leads us directly to another character, the relation of which to this is rather enigmatic, viz. 釿, *chin*.

Chin, 釿. This character appears, or seems to appear (the qualification will be explained below), on the so-called "money of Shun" (M. Lacouperie's Weight-Money), and on some archaic-looking round coins, figured *e.g.* in the Ku Ch'üan Hui, part 利, ch. i., pp. 4–6, and one in the "Catalogue," p. 327. The legends on these round coins, at any rate, show that it represents some unit of weight or value.

Now the character appears to cover more than one word. An analysis of the definitions and sounds given in the dictionaries shows that it is read both *chin* and *yin*.

When read *chin*, it is said to mean *axe* or *to cut with an axe*, and it does not seem unlikely, therefore, that the character is a mere variant of the simpler form 斤, and a second way of writing the same *word*.

But it has also the pronunciation *yin* (this both in the "upper even" and in the "rising" tones). In the latter, the Shuo Wên says it means *to cut into two parts*. (The Kuang Yün and Chi Yün dictionaries also attribute this sense to the character when read *chin*). When read *yin* in the upper even tone, there is still a third sense, that of a rasp or file for smoothing wood, "like a *t'ang*, 鍚," says the Liu Shu Ku, "but smaller."

If we assume that on the coins this is a single character, we may reasonably suppose also that we have to do with the sound *chin* meaning an axe, since that harmonises with the numismatic use of the form 斤, which has the same sound and sense.

M. Lacouperie does assume this, and here, at least, I incline to his opinion for the reason I am about to submit. But he gives no hint that there is any doubt about the matter. And there is grave doubt. So much indeed, that the authors of the Chin Shih So and the Ku Ch'üan Hui decline to treat this combination of strokes as one character, but as two, viz. *huo, object of exchange*, and *chin, metal*. The element which in 釿 forms the right-hand half, and at any rate appears to be the old form of 斤, *chin*, an *axe*, they consider to be really a distinct character, viz. an old form of 化 (= the modern 貨), *huo*.

What makes this a difficult theory to accept is that, although the need for economy of space might explain the two characters being packed closely together on the wedge-handled pieces, no such necessity existed with the round coins above referred to, and yet, in their case also, the two elements are juxtaposed even more closely than on the wedge-handled money. The inference seems to me cogent that one character and not two is in question.

Chin ch'ien, 金 錢. Metal money.

The expression is found in Kuan Tzŭ. Sometimes, as in the opening sentence of the already quoted passage from the Ch'ien Han Shu, both gold and copper are implied.

Chin pi, 金 幣. Metal treasure.

This expression occurs in Kuan Tzŭ, and may possibly have a wider scope than the previous one, and include mere ingots of metal.

Chin tao, 金 刀. Metal knives. See under *Tao ch'ien*.

Ch'ing chung, 輕 重. Relative weight or relative value.

This combination is very common in works on economic subjects or matters relating to coinage. A long section of the book known as Kuan Tzŭ is thus entitled, and "On Values," or even "On Economics" would be a fair rendering, considering the scope of its contents.

Where metal money is in question, it is well to remember that it is not so much mere weight, as what we should speak of as a high or a low denomination that is sometimes denoted.

Chou kuo, 周 郭. The surrounding rim or raised edge of a coin, whether *cash*, knife, or *pu* money.

Ch'üan, 權. The movable hanging weight of a balance, a balancing weight; figuratively, balance, equivalence; and as a verb, to balance or be equivalent to; to adjust the balance, to try the weight of, and figuratively, to estimate.

This word need not detain us long, but there is a peculiar phrase of which it forms part, that ought not to be passed over. One version of this is 子 母 相 權, *tzŭ mu hsiang ch'üan*, literally, "children and mother mutually balancing," that is the equivalence between a unit and the sum of its fractional parts.

In another shape the expression occurs near the beginning of the second part of the Food and Commerce Section of the Ch'ien Han Shu, in a passage quoted by Vissering on p. 25, and translated, but so imperfectly that a new rendering is necessary.

"The Emperor [Ching, of the Chou dynasty] was going

to cast large coins, and Tan Mu Kung said, 'It must not be. In old times Heaven sent down calamities. Then they reckoned their riches and estimated values, to save the people. If the people objected to the low value [*lit.* lightness] of the money, then they made for them money of a higher value, and put it in circulation. Thereupon they had '*the mother balancing the children*,' and the people were benefited. If the people were dissatisfied at the overhigh value of the current coin, then more coins of a smaller value were made and put in circulation, without abolishing the higher coin. In this way there were '*the children balancing the mother*' also in circulation, and both small and large coins were of use."

The expressions I have underlined are the literal rendering of the words 母權子, *mu ch'üan tzŭ*, and 子權母, *tzŭ ch'üan mu*, and can hardly mean anything else than an equivalence between a unit of given value and the sum of the fractional parts into which it was divided for purposes of currency, as though, for example, the English shilling were considered the 'mother,' and the penny the 'child,' — then the mother is equal in value to the twelve children.

Ch'üan, 泉. Closely involved with *ch'ien* as a numismatic term, we find the word *ch'üan*, either singly or combined with *pu* in the binomial 泉布, *ch'üan pü*.

The present and perhaps the primary meaning (if we are justified in assuming that we know the primary meaning of a word in any language) of *ch'üan* is a *spring of water*, or more precisely, according to the Liu Shu Ku, a deep pool fed by a spring, the spring itself being called 源, *yüan*.

"It is," says Tuan Yü-ts'ai in his note on the word in the Shuo Wên, "by extension that the ancients spoke of money as *ch'üan pu*."

The old form of the character was 𤼈, which the Liu Shu Ku considers pictorial.

M. Lacouperie correctly says (p. xvii.), "The term was used in ancient times for currency in general, and so far as it was paid in, not paid out." He notes its occurrence in the Chou Li, or Institutes of the Chou Dynasty, and that "One of the Treasuries of the Board of Finances derived his name, Tsiuen fu, 泉 府, from it."

Chêng K'ang-ch'êng, commenting on the section of the same work relating to the Wai Fu, or Office of the Exterior, which with the above-named Ch'üan Fu, had control of the money collected for the State, observes, "the term *pu*, 布 [currency], is equivalent to the term *ch'üan*. . . . Money when stored up was called *ch'üan*, when in circulation, *pu*, taking its name *ch'üan* from *shui ch'üan*, a *spring of water*, which flows in all directions. At first the *ch'üan* coins were of one sort only, but a second came into existence when Ching, Emperor of Chou, cast large coins, 大 泉."

Upon the identity of the *pu* with the *ch'üan* the native critics are in general agreed, as well as on the derivation of the latter term from the word meaning a *spring*, though they differ in their interpretations of the metaphor. Thus, Wang Shao-yü says: "The money as collected was called *pu*, when paid in to the Treasury it was styled *ch'üan*, for the word *pu* [literally, *spread* or *distribute*] expresses the fact of its spreading gain abroad, while *ch'üan* indicates that this gain issues from a single orifice (— 孔)," by which we are to understand presumably the spot where coins were cast, their place of issue.

Chêng Ngo writes: "Money—*ch'üan pu* as the Chou called it, *ch'ien* as we call it—was named *ch'üan* in allusion to its issuing as from a spring, and *pu* from its unchecked diffusion." Elsewhere the same scholar says: "If we inquire the reason for the terms applied to money, we shall find it denominated *ch'üan* from its issuing from a single orifice, and *pu*, because it spreads (布 散, *pu san*) throughout the realm. The money (錢 布, *ch'ien pu*) stored up in the Ch'üan Fu or Treasury was styled *ch'üan* and not *pu*, simply because the control over prices and over its storage or issue lies in the public authorities, just as a spring of water issues from a single opening."

A rather different interpretation of the term is that of

Li Shih-chên, the author of the great botanical work, the Pên Ts'ao Kang Mu, who is cited in the T'u Shu Chi Ch'êng Encyclopædia, as follows : " Under the Chou, T'ai Kung established the coinage (泉 法, *ch'üan fa*) of the Nine Treasuries. The coins, 泉 , *ch'üan*, were in structure circular with an inclosed square [hole], so many *shu* in weight, their complete circumfluent outline delineating a spring, for which reason they were so called." This extract illustrates that symbolizing tendency so dear to the Chinese mind, where it prevails perhaps as a necessary reaction from the grinding materialism of their daily life, like the backwaters in a rapid river.

Very different and very interesting is the account given by the great Sung dynasty critic, Chêng Ch'iao, or Chêng Chia-chi, as he is also called, from the place where he lived in retirement. Vissering (*Chinese Currency*, p. 8) has quoted the passage, omitting, however, thirty-one words near the beginning, for which reason, and because his rendering is otherwise faulty, I have made a fresh translation :—

" Money was called *ch'üan* in allusion to its outline ; *chin* [*metal*] in allusion to its material ; *tao* [*knife*] in allusion to the form given to it [器, *ch'i*] ; *huo* [*exchange*] and *pu* [*distribution*] in allusion to its functions. The word money, 錢, *ch'ien*, used to be, in the most ancient documents, written 泉. Then it [viz., the shape of money] was altered to the common knife, and then again to the *yüan fa* [or round *cash* ; a note on the text adds, 'which T'ai Kung made']. In that form it became generally diffused. The people approved of it, and accordingly, the *ch'üan* and knife-coins fell into disuse, and later generations did not have any knowledge of these terms. If we examine the ancient money, we find its shape is that of the Seal character for *ch'üan* [for which see the second paragraph of this entry], for which in after times the word *ch'ien*, 錢, was substituted. Hence the character 泉, *ch'üan* [no longer required or used for its original meaning of *money*], was borrowed to write the word *ch'üan* of *shui ch'üan*, a *spring of water.* The lower part of the true Seal character form of *ch'üan* does not consist of the character *water.* The early scholars, ignorant of the history of the character *ch'üan,* spoke of ' the onward flow of commodities being reflected in the *ch'üan,* their diffusion in the cloths, their high value in the gold, their utility in the knives.' Such a view is extremely forced."

There is both ingenuity and originality in this argument, frankly opposed as it is to the received opinions on the subject. We should, however, note two or three points arising from the statements expressed or implied by Chêng. On the one hand, it is true that the Seal form, at any rate the normal antique Seal form, as shown above, does not seem to be composed with the radical *water,* although the native dictionaries treat it as being so composed, even so independent an authority as the writer of the Liu Shu Ku concurring, and including *ch'üan* as a pictorial character. The picture, it must be confessed, is by no means convincing. On the other hand, I have met, so far, with no author agreeing with Chêng that the true and primary meaning of the term *ch'üan* was *money,* and that the same character was only used at a later date to transcribe an homophonous but distinct syllable signifying a *spring.* Chêng's words show moreover that he does not admit that the earlier forms of money were round, nor that *ch'üan* can be taken as equivalent to the *yüan fa,* as alleged by some. Far from that, he obviously identifies the former with the wedge-handled pieces classified by numismatists under the general designation *pu,* which we shall examine later.

Meanwhile a comparison of the Seal form of the character with two types of *pu* money illustrated in M. Lacouperie's Catalogue on pages 23 and 72 is instructive. The general likeness of outline, due allowance being made for the constraining effect of conventional treatment on a perhaps originally pictorial form, though not convincing, has a certain persuasive suggestiveness.

A scrutiny of the statements contained in the various

extracts already collected shows that they support the following propositions:—

1. A regular metallic currency, including both square plates of gold and circular copper pieces with a central square hole, was instituted at the foundation of the Chou dynasty, as tradition asserts, by the Minister known as T'ai Kung.

2. The threefold currency thus introduced is spoken of in the History of the Earlier Han dynasty as *yüan fa*, though the term has since been restricted to the copper coins only.

3. But these earliest copper *cash* were at first apparently called by another name, the exact form of which is open to some doubt, but which the balance of criticism inclines to show was first *ch'üan* and afterwards *ch'ien*.

4. If the substantial genuineness of the Chou Li is assumed, another denomination of this copper currency, namely *pu*, must have been in use either at the same time or soon afterwards.

This confronts us with the following difficulty: If the copper money was round and was called *ch'üan*, and if *pu* was merely another name for *ch'üan*, then the *pu* must have been round coins. Yet by general consent among the Chinese numismatic writers the *pu* are *not* the round but the wedge-handled and shouldered pieces. So, conversely, if the *pu* were of this last described type, and if *ch'üan* be a mere synonym of *pu*, then the *ch'üan* also could not have been round coins. Yet if the *ch'üan* were nothing else than *ch'ien*, which are expressly stated to have been originally, as now, round coins, then the *ch'üan* also must have been round.

Out of this apparent *impasse* I can see only three ways of escaping.

Assuming *ch'üan* and *ch'ien* to be identical, perhaps there were *some* that were not round coins. For example, Chêng Chia-chi may be right in declaring that *ch'üan* were earlier than, and of a different type from, the circular *yüan fa*, just as we know the knife-coins were.

Or secondly, there may have been some *pu* which were not of the wedge-handled shape now exclusively associated with that name by the numismatists, and such might have been circular. There is nothing in the name *pu*, or "currency," to limit the pieces so called to any special shape.

Or thirdly, the *ch'üan* and the *ch'ien* may *not* have been identical. It is conceivable that the *ch'üan* included both the knife and the wedge-handled types, and that when round coins were cast, a new designation—*ch'ien*—was also introduced for them. The use of both *ch'ien* and *ch'üan* in Kuan Tzŭ seems rather to make for this hypothesis, for it is hardly likely that the author would employ two distinct terms to describe exactly the same object.

There is one other explanation which would remove the difficulty, and that is to suppose the statement of the Chou Li is simply a wrong or at least an inadequate one. The genuineness of that work has of course been a vexed question.

Ch'üan fa, 泉 法. Coinage. This expression occurs in the Pên Ts'ao Kang Mu, in the passage quoted in the last entry, in place of the customary *yüan fa*. I have not met it elsewhere.

Ch'üan pi, 泉 幣. Metal money. A synonym of the next.

Ch'üan pu, 泉 布. Currency, literally "issue and currency."

"In ancient times," says a comment on the T'an Kung, "they spoke of money as *ch'üan pu*."

Hao, 好. The central hole in a *cash*. The much smaller hole pierced in some specimens of the *pi ch'êng ma* is also so called.

The original application of the term was to the similar central hole in the 璧, *pi*, or *jade token*. M. Lacouperie has evidently misread the latter character as 壁, *pi*, a *wall* or *screen*, for he renders *hao*, "*lit.* a hole in a wall."

Huo, 貨. Exchange; object or medium of exchange; article of commerce.

This is a frequent term in the literature relating to the

early history of money, especially in binomial combinations
with various other words.

The Shuo Wên briefly equates it with *ts'ai*, 財, *commodities, things of value.*

A comment on the Chou Li, cited in Kanghsi, explains
that "gold and jade are styled *huo*."

The first page of the opening chapter of the Section on
Food and Commerce in the History of the Earlier Han
dynasty has the statement, "*Huo* designates hempen cloth
and silk which can be used as clothes, as well as metal
knives and tortoise-shell, by means of which goods can
be divided, profit distributed, and commerce carried on."

In the Ku Ch'üan Hui, part 元, ch. 12, p. 2, Li Tso-
hsien writes: "*Huo* was anciently the general designation
of knife- and *pu*- coins."

The etymological history of the word is not without
interest. As will be remarked, the authorities quoted seem
to imply a fundamental identity, or at least a close kinship,
between *huo* and 化, *hua, to change.* In none of the
modern Chinese dialects, however, is a phonetic identity
to be now found. But in the Korean, Japanese, and
Annamese pronunciations of the two characters, the sounds
are the same.

The Kuang Yün dictionary says, "*Huo* signifies *hua*:
objects that are changed and converted: hence the character
contains [the element] *hua*."

In the Liu Shu Ku *huo* is always written 貨, the element
man being omitted, and the author thus discusses the word:—

"The signification of *huo* is *hua* [which he writes simply
七=化]: that by means of which commodities are exchanged and transported. Anciently written simply 七.
Exchange (*huo*) began with shells, hence the element 貝,
pei, shells, in the character. Money—*ch'ien*—and shells, gold
and jade, when exchanged in commerce, are termed *huo*."

Huo ch'ien, 貨 錢. Exchange money. This is the
phrase used in the Liu Shu Ku to explain *ch'üan*, 泉.

Huo pi, 貨 幣. Exchange treasure. This expression
seems restricted to the metallic money, or perhaps rather

ingots, alleged by traditions (which are preserved, for example, in the Lu Shih) to have been made by the mythical Fuhsi and Huang Ti. The Ku Ch'üan Hui contrasts *huo pi* with *yüan ch'ien* or round coins.

(1) *Huan,* 環 ⎫ This group of four characters,
(2)   „   鐶 ⎪ though not of special importance,
(3) *Yüan* or *Huan,* 瑗 ⎬ needs to be touched on, and the
(4) *Yüan,* 鍰 ⎭ sounds and meanings correctly
distinguished.

(1) *Huan,* 環. A ring of jade.

Such is the definition of the Yü P'ien dictionary. The Shuo Wên has, "A kind of *pi,* 璧, or token of jade." And the Erh Ya, describing the several varieties of the latter, says, "When the field and the hole are of equal breadth, the *pi* is called a *huan.*"

It was by this particular kind of ring that, according to Hsün Tzŭ, the Sovereign in old times used to recall to favour an official previously in disgrace.

The Liu Shu Ku asserts that this word was anciently written 8, representing two rings linked together.

The Erh Ya contains the curious statement that "knives were at first called *huan,* the shape being like rings," which no doubt refers to the ring-like extremities of the handles of the large knives of Ts'i, the former being called *huan.* Many examples are figured by M. Lacouperie in the "Catalogue," from p. 215 onwards.

In this connection it is worth quoting a curious and ancient example of that particular species of word-play, greatly affected by the Chinese, which may be described as a sort of pun round the corner. The Chin Shih So cites this instance from an old song. The line runs 何 日 大 刀 頭, that is, "On what day [will there be] a large knife end?" The end of the handles of the large knives of Ts'i consisted of a 環, *huan,* or *ring,* which has exactly the same sound and tone as the word 還, *huan,* to *return,* the character required for the sense, so that the speaker — doubtless a woman — says one thing, implies another, and means a third.

The character 環 is also interchanged with the third of this group, 瑗, in its reading of *huan*, and also with 圜, but only, apparently, when that is read *huan*.

(2) *Huan*, 鐶. A ring.

Defined by the Kuang Yün dictionary, cited in Kanghsi, as "a finger ring," while the Chêng Tzǔ T'ung says, "all circular discs having a hole to enable them to be strung together are known as 鐶, *huan*." This character does not appear either in the Shuo Wên or the Liu Shu Ku, which latter evidently treats the preceding form, 環, as the correct way of writing the word for 'ring.'

(3) *Yüan*, 瑗. A variety of the *pi* token.

According to the Shuo Wên, "a *pi* with a large central hole." The Erh Ya informs us that "when the hole is double the [breadth of the] field, [the *pi*] is termed a *yüan*."

This character is sometimes also read *huan*, and is then equivalent to 環.

(4) *Huan* or *Yüan*, 鍰. The name of an ancient weight.

The Shuo Wên defines this as equalling one *lüeh*, 鋝. (But the "Ssǔch'uan edition" has "six *lüeh*.") Another determination is that of K'ung An-kuo, who held that the weight meant was six ounces of "yellow iron," supposed by later scholars to be copper [see Legge's *Chinese Classics*, Shu King, vol. ii. p. 605].

Kanghsi adds, "Also, same as 環."

M. Lacouperie's rendering of this word on p. x. of the Introduction, and on p. 319, as "ring money," is unsupported by any of these authorities, as is his equation of it with 瑗, *yüan*.

Jou, 肉. "*Lit*. the flesh, *i.e.* the field of the piece," as M. Lacouperie says, Introduction, p. xx.

This term, with *hao*, the hole, and *chou kuo*, the rim, appears in the Section on Food and Commerce, of the History of the Earlier Han dynasty.

Jou hao, 肉 好. This expression does not have, as M. Lacouperie supposes, the same meaning as *hao* alone, but stands for "the field *and* the hole" of a *cash*.

Ku chu, 鼓 鑄. Literally, to smelt and cast; to cast coins. The first character does not mean, as M. Lacouperie says, a "smelting furnace," but, as Kanghsi explains, to make a fire blaze up by using a fan or bellows. On . p. xx. of the Introduction, the second character has not only been misprinted as *shou*, *old age*, but is also so transliterated.

Kuo, 郭. As M. Lacouperie says, "*lit.* a city wall, *i.e.* the raised edge." Often distinguished as *wai kuo*, the outer rim, and *nei kuo*, the inner rim, viz. that round the central hole.

Lai tzŭ, 來 子. The seed of the *lai* plant.

Under the Emperor known as Fei Ti, or "the Deposed," of the Liu-Sung dynasty, the debasement of the currency was extreme. Vissering has some account of the matter from Ma Tuan-lin, where the various derisive nicknames given to the wretched little *cash* by the people are mentioned, such as "Goose-eyes," 鵝 眼, *ngo yen*; "Fringe-rings," or perhaps "Thread-rings," 綖 環, *yen huan* (the allusion is not quite clear); others were called 來 子 or 萊 子, *lai tzŭ*, and 荇 葉, *hsing yeh*. The appropriateness of the latter name, "leaves of the *hsing* plant," is sufficiently shown by Bretschneider's description of this plant, *Limnanthemum nymphoides*—"The leaves are of a purplish red colour, they are orbicular (peltate), more than an inch in diameter. They float on the surface of the water." I have been unsuccessful in discovering what plant the "seeds of the *lai*" referred to, for the seeds of *chenopodium*, for which *lai* usually stands, do not appear to meet the required shape. There is one thing that is certain though, namely, that when Vissering, on p. 76, says these coins "were called fetus (來 子, *lit.* "coming children"), he took a wild leap in the dark, inasmuch as the Chinese themselves know nothing of any phrase of the sort either in the book language or the vernacular. M. Lacouperie has misprinted the character *lai* as 夾 [*chia*] on p. xix., but merely speaks of the term as "a sobriquet," in a wisely non-committal manner.

Lun kuo, 輪 郭 . Synonymous with *chou kuo, q.v.*

Man, 幕 . The reverse of a coin. Li Tso-hsien, in the Ku Ch'üan Hui, in view of the definition given in the Chi Yün dictionary, "flat and without characters," considers this term inapplicable to the reverses of coins having on that side a raised rim and an inscription. He, therefore, always employs the word 背, *pei, back.*

Nü ch'ien, 女 錢, and	Female money and
Kung shih nü ch'ien, 公 式 女 錢	Male-pattern Female money, respectively.

These are names given to an issue of 5-*shu* pieces of the Emperor Wu of the Liang dynasty, distinguished by having no raised rims, or only a rim round the central hole. According to a writer quoted in the Ku Ch'üan Hui, in Chapter VI. of the Section on Round Coins, those *cash* that had a raised rim round the hole on the reverse, were called *kung shih nü ch'ien*—freely translated, Hermaphrodite money; those that were destitute of any rim whatever, were called simply *nü ch'ien*, or Female money.

M. Lacouperie has, without authority, altered these terms, and made an imaginary 公 式 錢, *kung shih ch'ien*, which he translates "male money" (Introduction p. xix., and Catalogue p. 420), and wrongly states to be another name for the *nan ch'ien*, 男 錢, in contrast with the *nü ch'ien*. The true names, however, are as given above. See also the "Coins of the Southern Liang" in the Chin Shih So.

The *nan ch'ien*, or Male money, were *cash* with the legend 布 泉, *pu ch'üan*, issued probably by Wang Mang. According to Hung Tsun's Ch'üan Chih, cited in the Ku Ch'üan Hui, it was of these pieces that it was believed that a woman who wore one would have male offspring. Vissering, however, p. 83, relates this of some of the money of the Emperor Wu of the Liang dynasty, and M. Lacouperie in his entry, No. 54, Introduction p. xix., follows him, quoting him word for word, though without acknowledgment.

Pao huo, 寶 貨 . Valuable exchange.

We now come to a small group of perplexing questions, the best way of treating which seems to be to state the difficulties as clearly as possible, in the hope that solutions may be more easily reached, if distinct issues are raised.

Now we find in the Ch'ien Han Shu that "the Emperor Ching, finding the existing coins too light, cast new and larger pieces with the inscription *pao huo*."

We are also told by Hsün Yüeh in the Han Chi, as quoted in the Ku Ch'üan Hui, that under the Chou dynasty, money was inscribed and round, with a square central hole. Chêng Ch'iao is also quoted to the effect that the *yüan fa*, or circular coins of the Chou, had on them the word *huo*, *exchange*, thus showing, it is contended, that the designation on the money at the beginning of the Chou was *pao huo*. The Emperor Ching retained the inscription, but enlarged it to "4 *huo*" and "6 *huo*." Li Tso-hsien inserts figures of specimens inscribed simply *pao huo*, and others "*pao ssŭ huo*" and "*pao liu huo*" [four and six *huo*], and points out that the formation of the characters in all is identical, and incontestably belongs to Chou times.

Now in the well-known passage of the Ch'ien Han Shu recording the institution of a currency for the Chou by T'ai Kung, the commentator adds a note that the coins were one *ts'un* or inch [of that period, apparently, meaning, in diameter—the words are 圜 一 寸], and weighed nine ounces [of that period]. Ku Huan, a numismatic writer, assigns twelve *shu* as the weight. To both of these determinations the well-known writer Li Hsiao-mei takes exception. "How," he asks, "could coins weighing nine *liang*, or ounces, have been objected to in the reign of Ching as too light?" On the other hand, "if we suppose twelve *shu* to have been their weight, what addition to the latter was made by the new issue of his reign?" for the new pieces were of that very weight.

The author of the Ku Ch'üan Hui finds these two criticisms very just, but observes that Wêng I-ch'üan considers that the 12-*shu* pieces must refer to the *new* issue of the Emperor Ching. Li Tso-hsien then sums up all these statements, and deduces from them that the coins which Ching thought too light were the small pieces inscribed *pao huo*, the earliest coins of the dynasty; that the "new and enlarged coinage" indicates the *pao ssŭ huo* and *pao liu huo* pieces, while the words of the Ch'ien Han Shu, 子 母 相 權, literally "equivalence between sons and mother," refer to the sequence of coins of which the "sons" are the small *pao huo*, and the "mothers" the larger and heavier pieces that succeeded them.

Such is the view of Li Tso-hsien, whom M. Lacouperie well calls "one of the ablest and most sober of modern numismatists," but whose judgment in this matter he will not accept on the following grounds :—

"But," he objects on p. xxxvii., "this ingenious arrangement cannot be accepted : the latter coins, being inscribed, value 4 *huas*, value 6 *huas*, do not answer to the requirement concerning the innovation of *King Wang*; their mark indicates their relative value, and the actual weight of the specimens answers approximately to the standard weights ; they do not therefore weigh more than the market value of the time. Moreover, a double peculiarity in their make, *i.e.* their outside rims, and the fact that they were cast in clusters, show beyond any possible doubt that they were not coined before the fourth century B.C."

Now let us examine some of these statements.

The four and six *huo* coins, we are assured, "do not answer to the requirement concerning the innovation of *King Wang*." Why not? They are both heavier and larger than the simple *pao huo* coins. As for the "standard weights" and the "market value of the time," I have tried to understand M. Lacouperie's argument, but have not the faintest idea what he means. His next objection, however, is abundantly clear. The fact of these coins having an outside rim and being cast in clusters is fatal, in M. Lacouperie's eyes, to Li Tso-hsien's view. For, he says on p. lvi., they have rims, "sign of a later make which the others [viz. the *pao huo* coins] are without," and on p. 329 a rimless *pao huo* coin is figured. But M. Lacouperie

must have known and ought to have mentioned that Li
Tso-hsien expressly says, and shows by his illustrations,
that "both the field and the hole have surrounding rims"
(肉 好 俱 周 郭). The specimen in Mr. Gardner's
collection is probably a mere forgery and not a good one.
Thus the fact of the *pao liu huo* and *pao ssŭ huo* having
rims is rather in favour of Li Tso-hsien's argument than
otherwise.

The only support for the statement that the casting of
the *pao liu huo* and *pao ssŭ huo* in clusters disproves Li
Tso-hsien's view, is of the strictly "because it does" order.
M. Lacouperie says on p. xxxix., referring to the mould
for casting these coins, that the latter "have been incorrectly
attributed to TCHEOU *King*, in 523 B.C., by whom they
cannot have been issued." Why, he does not mention,
except to refer the reader to p. lvi. for "the reasons which
indicate their issue in Kiü *circ.* B.C. 350." The "reason"
given on that page is that "they were most probably
issued" there.

Whether the theory of the Ku Ch'üan Hui is right or
not, M. Lacouperie has brought nothing stronger than
assertions against it.

Another difficulty—its connection with the last will be
seen later—is the following :—

The knife-coins of Ts'i are the largest and finest of their
class, but we are only concerned now with their inscriptions.
On many of them are found on one side three large and
clearly cut characters in an abbreviated style. There is
no dispute about the first and third. All agree that they
represent the modern characters 齊, *ch'i* (Ts'i), and 貨,
huo, the first standing for the name of the State, the last
being one of the common terms for money. It is the
second word that forms a standing puzzle for numismatists
and antiquarians, and its very simplicity adds to its
difficulty.

In the first place it seems to be, or rather, so far as
form goes, it is, the old mode of writing 去, *ch'ü*, to
depart or *remove*. But as *ch'ü huo* is senseless, it is

generally agreed that *ch'ü* must be an abbreviation of some
more complex character, or characters, but the widest
divergence exists as to what the full form should be.

Let us examine first the theory advanced in the
" Catalogue," Introduction, p. xix., where M. Lacouperie
explains the symbol as " merely a simplified form of 弄,"
ch'ü, which he renders by " treasure," the binomial 去 化
meaning, according to him, " treasure to exchange," *i.e.*
" currency." The difficulty, however, in accepting this
supposition is that the assumed original, an exceedingly
rare word, does not appear to mean " treasure," as a
substantive, but only " to treasure," as a verb, if we may
judge from the only quotation given in Kanghsi. There
a passage from the Ch'ien Han Shu is adduced in which
the recipients of a certain personage's letters are said to
have admired the handwriting so much that they treasured
them up, 藏 弄, *ts'ang ch'ü*, as works of art. Of course
this word, like *ts'ang*, might have been used both as noun
and verb, but there is no evidence to show that it was,
besides that its extreme rarity greatly reduces the probability
of its use on coins.

The author of the Ku Ch'üan Hui believes that we have
to do with a shortened form of 法, *fa*, and he explains
that *fa huo* would mean legal or standard money. M.
Lacouperie says this cannot be, as *fa* " was not thus spelt
in former times," and declares that the word " is always
written " in a more elaborate form in old dictionaries and
texts. This is inaccurate. The shorter form 法 is added
in the Shuo Wên as a variant, and is also not infrequently
found in the text of that work.

But Li Tso-hsien's identification, though possible, is
perhaps a little far-fetched, and certainly not convincing.

Different, and very ingenious, is the explanation put
forward in the Ch'ien Chih Hsin Pien, 錢 志 新 編.
The author of this work would have us look upon the,
apparently, three characters as standing for four, viz.
齊 太 公 貨, or " Money of T'ai Kung of Ts'i," the two
sloping strokes of 太, *t'ai*, being made to do duty also

as the two upper strokes of 公, *kung*, the apparently simple character 厺, *ch'ü*, thus being really the above two characters welded together, a process, he declares, often met with on knife and *pu*-coins.[1]

One obvious objection to this theory is that there would not be sufficient motive for the abbreviation, where space was so ample as on these knives. But the force of the objection is somewhat lessened if Li Tso-hsien (who does not hold this theory) is right in supposing that the knives with three characters are later than those with four and six, as it might be argued that the economy of space necessary at first, was continued from mere use and habit.

There seems little to be said in favour of reading the character as a variant of 合, *ho*, *harmony*, and an identification with 吉, *chi*, *lucky*, which in point of conformation is very near, is negatived by the fact that on some of these knife-coins both *chi*, *lucky*, and the character under discussion occur together and are perfectly distinct.

There remains the proposal of the Ch'ien Shih T'u and the Chin Shih So to take 厺 as an old form of 寶, *pao*, *valuable*, the whole legend in this way reading *Ts'i pao huo*, or Money of Ts'i.

The author of the latter work asserts positively that the character usually read *ch'ü* was an old form of *pao*. Of course if he is right, *cadit quæstio*. But such a form is not to be found in the Shuo Wên, the Liu Shu Ku, or the Liu Shu T'ung. Moreover, the form of *pao huo cash* discussed above is not the same nor at all similar, and though that alone is not fatal to the interpretation, it affords it no support.

For the present, then, the data seem insufficient to solve the question, which is one of considerable epigraphic interest.

Pi, 幣. Treasures, objects of value.

---

[1] In our own Office of Works the passion for economy is carried out in such an unfaltering spirit that the V.R. marked on Government furniture, boundary stones, etc., is carved thus ℜ, a single line serving as the right-hand stroke of the V and the upright of the R.

This is a common and important word in all that relates to the monetary system of the ancient Chinese. It is curious that the Shuo Wên defines it simply as "silks," 帛. The Liu Shu Ku is rather fuller, and we read that "silks which are used in friendly intercourse are called *pi*: money and shells are thence also termed *pi*."

So too, the great scholar Chêng K'ang-ch'êng (cited in Kanghsi under the word 布, *pu*), commenting on a passage in the Odes, declares that "*pi* is what is used to buy with. This word *pi* is a general term for objects of exchange (貨), such as clothes and silks and metal money."

And Kanghsi quotes one authority who specifies gold, jade, ivory, hides, and metal money (泉 布, *ch'üan pu*) as *pi*; and another who includes horses among tributary *pi*; and a third who adds weapons to this list.

M. Lacouperie, therefore, well renders the word on p. ix. by "valuables (*i.e.* metal implements or commodities easy to barter)."

In numismatic works the word has usually a more restricted sense. It serves there as a generic term for any of the early forms of metal money. The binomial 錢 幣, *ch'ien pi*, is the fuller expression in this usage.

Kuan Tzŭ has a passage running, "Yü with metal from the Li mountains cast *pi* to relieve men's distress." The same statement is also found in the Lu Shih. "This," says the author of the Pên T'sao Kang Mu, who quotes Kuan Tzŭ, "was the beginning of money, 錢."

It seems rather surprising that a word meaning specially silks, as we are told, and written, be it remarked, with the radical 巾, *chin*, a *cloth*, should have been applied, and that at an early period, to metallic money. Certainly there exists another form of the character, where the radical *cloth* is replaced by 貝, *pei*, a *shell*, which appears a more suitable classifier for such a general term. This variant is not found in the Shuo Wên, though given in the next earliest dictionary, the Yü P'ien, dating from the sixth century A.D., and in the Lei P'ien. The former work states that the form 幣 is the more modern one.

Pi ch'eng ma, 幣乘馬 "Team money."

Ch'êng ma pi, 乘馬幣   „

Ch'êng ma huo, 乘馬貨   „

Ts'ê ma huo, 策馬貨 "Reckon horses money."

Ts'ê ch'êng ma, 策乘馬 "Reckon teams."

Ts'ê ch'êng ma pi, 策乘馬幣 "Reckon teams treasure."

Tang chin huo, 當金貨 "Equal to *chin* money."

Tung chin ts'ê ch'êng ma, 當金策乘馬 "Equal to *chin* reckon teams."

Shun pi, 舜幣 "Shun's treasure."

The full explanation of these grotesque-looking terms will be found further on. Meantime it will be sufficient to say that the objects to which the names are applied, the legends inscribed on them, and even the names themselves, furnish the hardest tangle of obscurities and difficulties to unravel that confronts us anywhere in this branch of inquiry.

In order to clear the ground, a good deal of destructive criticism will be necessary, inasmuch as M. Lacouperie has further perplexed an already perplexing subject by some gratuitous and serious errors.

His observations (Introduction, p. xviii.) are as follows :—

"16. 幣乘馬 *Pi tch'eng ma,* Saddle money ;

16. 車馬 *Kiu ma,* same meaning ;

18. 筴策馬 *Kia tseh ma,* Slip-weight money ;

19. 策馬 *Ts'eh ma,* same meaning.

Appellatives of a curious shape of copper money, bearing its weight value, and the name of its place of issue, from the seventh to the fourth century B.C."

To this must be added the subjoined passage on p. 18 of the "Catalogue," under the heading of "Weight-Money."

"Tchang-I 張儀, who was Prime Minister in Tchao until 357 B.C., was granted by his sovereign Su 肅 (348–325 B.C.) the privilege of issuing *Kiü-ma* 車馬 money. Such was one of the appellatives of this class of currency. Another one was *Pi tch'eng ma* 幣乘馬, or 'Riding Money,' so called from its likeness of shape to that of a saddle. But the oldest was *Kia ts'eh ma,* 筴策馬, or better *Ts'eh ma*, 策 碼, 'Slip-Weight Money,' whence Weight-Money."

Thus M. Lacouperie. Now for a methodical examination of his statements.

16. *Pi ch'êng ma* cannot possibly mean Saddle money, and in so naming it M. Lacouperie has supplied a conjectural reason for an imaginary fact. It could, however, have meant "riding money," if the second word of the phrase were in the 'lower even' tone, for *ch'êng ma* then means *to mount a horse*, but, as we shall see, the word is to be read in the 'departing' tone, and then the meaning of *ch'êng ma* is *a team of four horses*.

17. No such expression as 車 馬, *chü ma*, is applied to any form of money. This is one of the worst of the errors into which the author of the "Catalogue" has fallen. I shall return to it shortly.

18. I believe I am correct in saying that no such phrase as 筴 策 馬 is to be found, but that it is in some way due to a confusion on M. Lacouperie's part, arising from the word *ts'é*, 策, being sometimes written 筴, the normal sound of which is *chia* (*kia*), but which when used for 策 also takes the same sound—*ts'é*. But had such a phrase existed, it could not possibly mean "slip-weight money," if indeed those three words convey any meaning, which to me they do not.

19. *Ts'eh ma*, 策 馬, has the same meaning, we are told. But on p. 18 we find this phrase "better" written 策 碼. What does M. Lacouperie mean by "better"? Neither in Kuan Tzŭ, whence the actual terms are derived, nor in any of the coin books I have examined, is *ts'é ma* ever written with the character 碼, which does mean a *weight*, whereas 馬 means a *horse*. *One* of the two must be chosen. Both cannot be right. If 馬, a *horse*, be selected, a *weight* must be abandoned; if 碼, a *weight*, be chosen, the authority should be given, for it is altogether inconsistent with the history of the term, as I shall show shortly.

But before doing this, we must go back to the words *chü ma*, literally "carriage and horses," which for the moment stop the way. The explanation is very simple, and M. Lacouperie had little reason for falling into so disastrous an error.

Besides the passage quoted above from p. 18, the author writes on p. lii. of the Introduction, " the king of Tchao issued *kiü ma* currency (發 金 幣 車 馬) or saddle money, and granted the use (奉 以 車 馬 金 錢) of it to Tchang Y, a political adventurer from Ts'in, where he returned in 317 B.C." A statement in the same sense appears on p. xiv. under the years 325–317 B.C.

The two passages which M. Lacouperie quotes are from the original narrative in the Chang I Chuan, or Memoirs of Chang I, in the Shih Chi. Not only has he completely misunderstood the text, but he has mistaken the fundamental facts of Chang I's relations to the States of Chao and Ts'in.

Chang was never " Prime Minister in Chao," nor was he, when he came to that State, an " adventurer from Ts'in," nor did the Prince of Chao ever grant him " the privilege of issuing " money.

Chang I came as a penniless adventurer to Chao to seek his friend and former fellow-student, Su Ts'in, who, and not Chang, was Prime Minister to the Prince of that State. Su did not give the new-comer the welcome he looked for, and Chang left the country to try his fortunes in Ts'in. Su Ts'in seems to have desired that Chang should succeed in gaining access to the ruler of Ts'in, and as that would have been difficult for a needy adventurer, he used his influence with the Prince of Chao in the way explained in the following passage from the above-mentioned Memoirs:

趙 王 發 金 幣 車 馬 使 人 微 隨 張 儀 與 同 宿 舍 稍 稍 近 就 之 奉 以 車 馬 金 錢 所 欲 用 爲 取 給 而 弗 告 張 儀 遂 得 以 見 秦 惠 王

" The Prince of Chao gave out money (金 幣), and a carriage and horses (車 馬), and sent a messenger to follow Chang I unobserved, to lodge in the same places as he, and gradually to grow intimate with him, putting at his disposal (奉) the carriage and horses and the money (金 錢), and providing for him whatever he might stand in want of, without telling him [probably, " who had really provided it," should be understood]. In this way Chang I was able to gain access to Prince Hui of Ts'in."

Never, surely, have a carriage and horses been put down and turned into money, to meet a less urgent necessity!

For the true explanation of these terms we must turn to the works of Kuan Tzŭ, where, in the Section entitled Ch'ing chung, or Economics, the clue is to be found.

Put in the briefest possible way, the facts are these: Native numismatists have identified certain forms of the *pu* type of money as surviving examples of the *pi*, or metal "treasures," said by Kuan Tzŭ to have been used by the Emperor Shun in connection with his system of taxation and administration. To that system Kuan Tzŭ gives the name of 筴 乘 馬 之 數, *ts'ĕ ch'ĕng ma chih shu*, shortened sometimes to *ts'ĕ ch'ĕng ma*, which expressions mean literally, " to devise, or the devising of, the scheme of teams of horses." This again may be interpreted either in a literal sense, which on the whole seems to me the more natural, as the system [of taxation] based on teams of horses; or, as the Chinese critics themselves seem to prefer, the words may be taken figuratively as the management of the team of State by the Imperial driver, in which case *ts'ĕ* must be given its meaning of a *switch*, or to *use a switch*. As I hope to show, this fiscal system was one in which a definite area of cultivated land was assessed as liable to provide one chariot and four horses fully equipped for the armed forces of the State.

If the Ch'ing chung Section is from the hand of Kuan Tzŭ, or even if it embodies and combines genuine older materials, the contents deserve attention as an outline—and often more than that—of the agrarian policy of the pre-historic dynasties believed to have preceded that of Chou, and to have witnessed under the legendary Emperor Shun the first beginnings of the use of money. I trust then it may not be out of place to append here a close paraphrase of the opening chapter of this Section on " Economics," the less so as the function of *pi* or *treasure*, probably in some metallic form, is also illustrated.

The text is thrown into the form of dialogue between the Duke Huan of the State of Ts'i and his Minister Kuan, generally styled in this work Kuan Tzŭ.

The Duke asks Kuan Tzŭ to explain to him the *ch'êng ma.*

The Minister replies in that oracular manner which might in these hurrying times be deemed irritating, but which seems to have enjoyed considerable vogue in days of yore, "The State's lack of stores comes from the Ruler's commands."

"How so?" inquires the Duke.

"One farmer," is the reply, "can only till a hundred *mou* of land. The labours of Spring are limited to the twenty-five days."

"And what are the twenty-five days?"

Kuan Tzŭ replies: "Sixty days after the winter solstice, the surface of the ground thaws; seventy days after, the ground below the surface thaws. Then the farmer sows his millet. After one hundred days from the solstice, he ceases sowing. Thus the labours of Spring are limited to twenty-five days. The Rulers of these times now build Palaces, and the people all have to work at them. If Spring is allowed to pass without stopping the work, the people lose 'the twenty-five days,' and all the land from which they are drawn will be neglected land. If one man is forced to work at this *corvée*, a hundred *mou* go untilled; if ten men, then a thousand *mou*, and so on. After Spring is past, there are Rulers who still exact *corrée* in the Summer. In this way, the fruits alike of Spring. and Summer are lost. When *corvée* is not stopped even in Autumn, then the saying applies that 'crops and land are lost several times over.' When the season has passed without crops, the merciless Ruler still exacts his taxes. The share of the harvest required to feed the people is five-tenths, and the Ruler has already exacted nine-tenths, and sometimes even, in default of grain, will cruelly demand treasure (幣, *pi*) instead. It is by such conduct that lawlessness arises and penalties abound."

"Excellent!" somewhat hurriedly observes the Duke, and continues, "Pray explain fully to me the policy of the *Ts'è ch'éng ma* (策乘馬之數)."

"Those Rulers [*i e.* of antiquity]," answers the Minister, "did not take the time of the people, and so the crops were plentiful, the officials (士) needed but light salaries, and the people but scanty donations. The wise Rulers of those times caused the farmers to plough in the winter and to weed in the summer, and fruits of their labours fell to the Ruler. The women being diligent at their needlework, their weavings accrued to the Treasuries. The motive for this [levy on the produce of men and women's toil] was not to grieve or afflict the people, but because the scheme of fiscal control required that thus it should be."

The Duke then asks how such a policy may again be carried out.

His Minister answers: "In the State of Yü [有虞國— the native State of Shun] was devised the system of *Ch'éng ma*. That system was one of grants made to the man of a hundred *mou*." [There here seems to be a lacuna in the text, which continues as though the ancient Ruler—perhaps Shun—were addressing the people.] "'In general, the twenty-seven [*sic*] days are the time of your Spring labours, and of assisting you with treasure (幣). When your Spring and Autumn harvests are plentiful, the State's share of your grain will be a heavier levy.' Addressing the farmers [*sic*], he said, 'The value of the treasure (幣, *pi*) in your hands will be reckoned in grain and stored in the district granaries. The share of the grain due to the State is first and foremost [? 在上, *in orig.*]. The importance of that share is tenfold, as providing the salary of the various officials of all sorts. When implements and arms are furnished in full, then a State exists. In the absence of treasure, the equivalent in grain is fixed. Of the State's provision for contingencies [? literally, screens], 90 per cent. consists of grain repaid [as taxes] to the State,

and of grain to meet [expenses]. Arms being fully provided, there is no further levy for them from the people.'
Such was the *ts'ê ch'êng ma* of Yu Yü."

To this passage I must add another short one from the
ninth chapter of the same Section. Translated, it runs as
follows :—

"Duke Huan asked Kuan Tzǔ as to the *pi ch'êng ma*
(幣 乘 馬).

"Kuan Tzǔ replied : 'At first taxes were levied from the
establishments of the three grades of Great Officers
(三 大 夫 之 家), one chariot and team of horses with
twenty-seven men to serve it for each piece of land of six
square *li* [? 方 六 里]. As to the *pi ch'êng ma*, if a piece
of land of that size were of such and such a quality, the
yield of grain would be of such and such a quantity, and
the value of the grain of such and such an amount. For
each such area of land, then, so many treasures, or *pi*, were
used [presumably in payment of the tax], and according
to the heaviness of the crop upon it [also], so many *pi*.
Hence by this *pi ch'êng ma* system, these *pi* were distributed
throughout the State, were a measure of the cultivable
land of the realm, and were known by the name of *pi
ch'êng ma*.'"

It remains to analyse the various terms at the head of
this entry, which designate the supposed survivors of these
ancient treasure-tokens.

The first is *pi ch'êng ma*, a strange-looking compound, for
the syllable *pi*, which I believe is never found except as
a substantive, seems, at any rate at first sight, to be used
adjectively here, and even so the expression is difficult to
explain. The clue appears to be given in the following
sentence, which occurs a little further on than the passage
last referred to: 枋 國 之 筴 貨 幣 乘 馬 者 也.
Slightly expanded, this means, "the plan which serves as
the cross-piece to the pole of the car of State [that is, which
enables the driver to control the horses, or, in other words,
the *sine quâ non* of continuous existence as a State] is the
huo pi ch'êng ma system."

Here, instead of the previous *pi ch'êng ma*, we have the fuller and more intelligible combination *huo pi ch'êng ma*, which appears to stand for " metal currency (*huo-pi*) and the [system of taxation known as] *ch'êng ma*."

Ch'êng ma pi and *Ch'êng ma huo*, which occur in coin-books, are, of course, nothing but " money of the *ch'êng ma* system."

Ts'ê ch'êng ma pi, or *Ts'ê ch'êng ma*, or *Ts'ê ma huo*, various forms of the same term, are names based on the statement as to Shun's taxation already quoted above, where the alternative explanations of the phrase are given.

Tang chin huo (and in the Lu Shih, *Tang chin ts'ê ch'êng ma*). This name has come into use from the fact that the two characters 當 金, *tang chin*, in the old script, are found on many of the pieces of this type. The current opinion among the native writers is that the *chin* here refers to a unit of value, which has already been discussed under a separate entry.

Shun pi, or " Shun's treasure," explains itself.

On the whole, the evidence seems to me insufficient to decide whether these curious pieces with their enigmatic legends are rightly identified with the *pi* or *treasure* which Kuan Tzŭ describes as in use in Shun's time. They have a very archaic look, but the true reading of the inscriptions is still exceedingly doubtful. It appears not unlikely, however, that they offer us the oldest form of the *pu* type that has come down to our times. It would be interesting to discover what that form represents.

Po hsüan, 白 撰. Meaning somewhat uncertain, but probably, " White and choice."

Among various coins issued by the Emperor Wu of the Han dynasty, there were three types known to numismatists apparently by tradition only, and called respectively Dragon-money, Horse-money, and Tortoise-money. They are described as being made of an amalgam of silver and tin. The Dragon-money was round, symbolizing Heaven, and having the figure of a Dragon encircling a central round hole. The name, it is recorded in the Section on Food and Commerce of the Ch'ien Han Shu, was *Po hsüan*, the import of which is probably as rendered above.

Vissering, *On Chinese Currency*, p. 40, gives the traditional illustrations of the three coins, as well as the text relating to them from Ma Tuan-lin, but he reads 曰, *yüeh, to say*, instead of 白, *po, white*. This is also the reading in some texts in the Ch'ien Han Shu, but not that followed by the editors of Kanghsi, who have 名 白 撰, *ming po hsüan*, "it was named *Po hsüan*." Vissering translates, "its name shall be *tšuan*" (a wrong transliteration, as a reference to Kanghsi shows), adding in a note that the word "has the signification of regulator, a pattern." It has no such meaning. M. Lacouperie has, again without acknowledgment, closely followed Vissering in this error. On p. xix. of the Introduction, he has "撰, *Tchuan*, pattern," and words to the same effect on p. 358, in both cases omitting all mention of the first part of the name.

Pu, 布. (1) Cloth, (2) Currency.

The treatment of the term *pu* requires some little care, because it appears in connection with the early history of money in two senses which need to be sharply distinguished. The first of these senses, and the only one mentioned in the Shuo Wên, is that of *hempen cloth*. The second is that of a *metallic currency*.

It is, according to Kanghsi (*s.v.* 布), synonymous with *ch'üan*, 泉, in the sense of money, and Yen Shih-ku is quoted to the same effect,—"*pu* is the same as *ch'ien*. It is so termed to express its distribution (分 布) and general currency."

Vissering is confused and misleading in regard to this word of double functions, and M. Lacouperie also, in some degree, fails to observe the distinction sufficiently.

The Shuo Wên and the Liu Shu Ku both consider the meaning of "cloth" to be the original one, and the latter asserts that the character was 'borrowed' to write the *pu* in *chan pu* (展 布), *to spread out, unfold*, and in *hsüan pu* (宜 幣), *to spread abroad, proclaim*, whence it came also to be used for the *pu* in *huo pu* (貨布), *currency of exchange*, from the meaning of *diffusion* or *distribution* (流 布), borne by that term. So, too, Tuan Yü-ts'ai, in his notes on *pu* in the Shuo Wên, holds that the general sense of *distribution* is derived by extension from that of *cloth*.

It is more likely, however, that the reverse is the case, and that the original sense of *pu* is the general one, equivalent to our word *spread*. Of this, "cloth," or literally "spreading," as a term for a fabric with a certain spread of surface, would be a particular application. And a currency of metal would be a second specialized use of the parent word, applicable to any form of money, from its widespread diffusion as a circulating medium.

Vissering has not realised this. Thus on p. 3 of his work he translates Ma Tuan-lin's 商 人 齊 人 謂 之 布 by "the people of *Sang* and *Ts'i* called it Pu, a hempen or silk piece of cloth," and immediately afterwards, "The money of the first three dynasties . . . was made of three different sorts of metal, yellow, white, and red, and consisted further of cloth, knives, and tortoise-shells." In both instances it is clearly the metallic *pu* that are intended to be understood.

M. Lacouperie has the following entry, on p. xviii.: "*Pu*, cloth, afterwards money. First applied to hempen or silk pieces of cloth. Used as a medium of exchange and regulated into a currency in 1091 B C., it [*sic*, Qy. the term] came into use in a looser way as money, and was especially applied to all small plates of metal employed for currency, except the knives. It is chiefly applied by numismatists to the small shape of money derived from the spade and saddle money." On the same page, he translates *huo pu* by "exchangeable (cloth) money," and *ch'ien pu* by "hoes and cloth"; so, on p. xii., "*Pus* (hoes or adzes)," while on p. 32, speaking of these *pu*-coins, he says, "Their name *pu*, 布, which means 'spread out,' was used in olden times for this money in the Ts'i State."

So far as I can follow M. Lacouperie, I suppose him to consider that the term *pu* means cloth, but that the metal shape to which the term was applied represents a hoe or an adze.

Now it may again be pointed out that we learn from the Ch'ien Han Shu that there was a medium of exchange consisting of pieces of hempen cloth, and also of silk, of definite size, forty Chinese feet in length, and two feet two inches in breadth. It is to these ancient "piece-goods" that the common expression 布 帛, *pu po*, or "cloths and silks," is applied.

But when a currency of copper is denominated *pu*, it assuredly cannot be associated with such cloths. Could there be a more infelicitous name for a small piece of metal money than "a cloth"? Vissering does indeed put forward an explanation, but, so far as I am aware, it is not supported by any historical evidence. He says on p. 4: "Hempen and silk cloth and knives were the earliest articles of trade generally used for money, and as the first weighed metallic money was an imitation of the shape and a representation of those articles, the same denominations remained to designate those coins. The *pu*-coins represent a piece of cloth, a dress, and the *tao*-coins are in their outward form an imitation of a sword or knife." He further thinks that the likeness between the character 布 and the form of the coin so named can be traced. Vissering's statement that the first "metallic money was an imitation of the shape and a representation of" knives, seems probable enough, but surely not of a piece of cloth (for *pu* does not mean "a dress"). We are told exactly the dimensions of the cloths, which were long strips of uniform breadth, whereas the *pu*-coins are wedge-handled, shouldered plates, the lower part of which is broader than the handle. The latter is usually pierced, and the lower edge of the coin is always interrupted by a deep wedge-shaped or elliptical opening, as may be seen in M. Lacouperie's abundant illustrations of the series. If the *pu* are imitations in metal of strips of cloth, how are these peculiarities of design to be explained? Whatever may have suggested the shape of these odd-looking coins, it can hardly have been a simple length of

cloth.   The coincidence of the name is probably responsible
for Vissering's hypothesis, and one may surmise that Chêng
Chia-chi's ingenious theory as to the *ch'üan* has also had
something to do with it.   In fact, however, these very
pu-coins seem to be the "ancient coins" to which Chêng
refers as originating the old seal-character form of *ch'üan*.

Accepting as beyond dispute the meaning of "metal
currency" for *pu*, we may note that in the Chou Li it is
by this designation only that money is spoken of, unless
we except the title of *Ch'üan fu*, or Treasury of Money,
where alone we meet the word *ch'üan*.   Further, the Ku
Ch'üan Hui (vol. i. 凡 例, p. 2) represents Kuan Tzŭ
apparently as stating that at the beginning of the Chou
dynasty, *yüan fa* (which the K.C.H. always treats as round
coins) were called *pu*.   I have not found this statement
in Kuan Tzŭ, but it may be there.

M. Lacouperie in his "Catalogue" has made a separate
division for certain specimens of early money to which he
has given the title of "Weight-Money."   The pieces of
this type in Chinese coin-books are, with others, often
styled 異 布, *i pu*, that is, exceptional or unusual *pu*.   There
are other names which are discussed under the entry *Pi
ch'êng ma*, but to my thinking it would have been better
to have treated these coins as a subdivision of the *pu*
than to set up a separate class for them.   The so-called
"Weight-Money" bears a strong general resemblance to
the ordinary *pu*-coins, being usually distinguished by having
rounded instead of angular shoulders, and a conical or
segmental concavity replacing the wedge-shaped opening
of the normal *pu*.   But the type seems the same, and we
may perhaps regard M. Lacouperie's "Weight-Money" as
the archaic predecessor of the angular *pu*.

As we have already seen, M. Lacouperie asserts that the
pu are hoes, but he does not attempt to meet the obvious
objection that they do not resemble the Chinese hoe, nor to
account for the very characteristic opening in the lower edge.

I venture to put forward the following theory as a possible
explanation in the absence of any other.   It involves an

examination of two terms, *ch'iao* and *ch'a*, which occur both separately and also in a binomial combination. These are names of two ancient implements of tillage very similar, it would seem, in function. When the binomial is used, it probably stands not for " the *ch'iao* and the *ch'a*," but for the *ch'iao* variety of the *ch'a*, the latter term being generic. The character 鏺, *ch'iao*, is not in the Shuo Wên; but in the Liu Shu Ku it is defined as " a sort of 鈶, *ch'a*. Used to shovel away earth and other things." In combination, as noticed above, we have 鏺 鈶 as a distinct term.

As for 鈶, *ch'a*, it is a character with two meanings. In the Shuo Wên it is described as a pestle for husking grain. But this alleged meaning is not represented in literature, at least, no example is cited in Kanghsi. *Ch'a*, however, has also the meaning of a spade or shovel, a fact which Tuan Yü-ts'ai explains as due to ' borrowing.' And the Shuo Wên itself, though silent as to this sense when defining the word, repeatedly defines other terms for implements of the nature of spades or shovels, as 鈶 屬 也, " a sort of *ch'a*." In fact, as will be seen under the character *ch'iao* in Kanghsi, *ch'iao* and *ch'a* are synonyms, but are used in different localities.

Now in the Shantung sculptures which form the subject of M. Chavannes' fine work, "*La sculpture sur pierre en Chine*," and which have also been very well reproduced in the Chin Shih So, we find in several instances an implement represented to which I would draw attention. It looks like an abortive tuning-fork, or a hybrid between a two-pronged fork and a spade. One example occurs in the ninth panel of the chamber of the "pseudo-Ou Léang," where the Emperor Yü is figured holding it in his right hand. M. Chavannes calls it merely " un instrument aratoire," but the authors of the Chin Shih So in their notes on their woodcut describe it as a 鏺 鈶, *ch'iao ch'a*. We meet it again twice in the curious sets of figures forming the third row of the first stone of the Posterior Chambers (Chavannes, plate xxix.). In the Chin Shih So the pictures represent the figures on a white background, and are therefore far more distinct than the plates in M. Chavannes' volume. The authors of the Chinese work here describe the winged personages who hold this implement as "grasping a two-bladed *ch'a* (兩 刃 臿, *liang jên ch'a*)," not, as in the previous instance, a *ch'iao c'ha*.   Now these words *liang jên ch'a* form the Shuo Wên's definition of the spade-shaped instrument known as a *hua*, and in modern times (but not in the Shuo Wên) written 鏵.   Tuan Yü-ts'ai, in a long and valuable note, has these observations—"The words 'two-bladed *ch'a*' mean a *ch'a* both sides of which have an edge (or blade).   A *ch'a* is an implement for cutting into the soil."   This interpretation would agree with the illustration of a *hua* given in the T'u Shu Chi Ch'êng better than with the view of the authors of the Chin Shih So, who presumably see in the two flattened prongs the "two blades" mentioned by the Shuo Wên.

But for my argument it does not matter whether the implement figured is a *hua*, a *ch'iao ch'a*, or some other. That an agricultural tool of such a shape did exist once is certain from these sculptures, and the conclusion I venture to suggest is that in this implement, whatever its name and exact use, we have the formal origin of the *pu*-coins.

Pu ch'üan, 布 泉.   Currency.

This expression, the ordinary phrase *ch'üan pu* reversed, was not only the legend on one of the various kinds of *pu* issued by Wang Mang, but it also occurs in Kuan Tzŭ, *e.g.* in ch. 24, p. 9—"The nobles of the Empire brought gold, gems, grain, ornamental fabrics (文 采, *wên ts'ai*), and currency (布 泉, *pu ch'üan*), to pay to Ts'i in exchange for its stone tokens (石 璧, *shih pi*)."

Shên lang ch'ien, 沈 郎 錢.   Sir Shên's money.

Very small *cash*—some are hardly larger than a silver penny—were cast under the Tsin dynasty, by a personage named Shên Ch'ung, 沈 充.   The Ku Ch'üan Hui extracts the following passages relating to their issue :—

"The Section on Food and Commerce in the History of the Tsin dynasty records that at Wu Hsing [now

Huang Chou fu in Chehkiang], Shên Ch'ung also cast small *cash* known as *Shên lang ch'ien*, or Sir Shên's money."

The second passage, from the Chi Chin Lu, runs thus: "The Emperor Ming, of the Wei dynasty, resumed the coinage of the 5-*shu* pieces, which continued in use until the Tsin dynasty. Shên Ch'ung, however, lessened their size while keeping the same inscription."

Such is the commonplace story of the designation of these diminutive coins. Vissering does not allude to them; but M. Lacouperie has this brief and staggering entry, on p. xix. of the Introduction—

"49. 不 沈 郎 *Puh tch'én lang*, unsinkable lads."

Having supplied the negative, *pu*, which does not form part of the name, and omitted the word *ch'ien*, *money*, which does, and taken 沈 in its meaning of "sink," and its sound *ch'én* (*tch'én*), instead of correctly reading it *shén*, a surname, he finally renders *lang* by "lads" (a meaning the character often has), whereas it is really here a suffixed honorific. Surely the restoration has been carried rather far in this case!

Tao, 刀, or *Chin tao*, 金 刀, or *Tao ch'ien*, 刀 錢, or *Tao pi*, 刀 幣. Knives, or Metal knives, or knife money, or knife-treasure.

This curious variety of coin, if that term may be applied to it, forms the third of the types into which all Chinese copper money falls.

Kuan Tzŭ speaks of gold and "knife-treasure," *tao pi*, circulating among the people (Ch'ing-chung, Section 6), and of *tao pu*, "knives and *pu* money," being stored in the official treasuries (*loc. cit.*, Section 9, folio 25). And in numismatic works the knives are constantly associated with the *pu*-coins in the expression *tao pu*, "knives and *pu*," as distinguished from the round *cash*—*chin ch'ien* or *yüan fa*. Thus the P'ing Chun Shu Section of the Shih Chi says, "When the way of commerce was first opened to husbandmen, craftsmen, and traders, valuables of tortoise-shell, metal coins (金 錢), and knives and *pu* (刀 布) came into use."

On the first page of the Section on Food and Commerce
in the Ch'ien Han Shu, we find mention of "metal knives
and tortoise-shell, with which wealth was divided and gain
distributed."

The Ku Ch'üan Hui cites the T'ung Chih, or Memoirs
of? Ssŭ-ma Ch'ien, for the statement that money was known
as "knives" in the States of Ts'i and Chü, which occupied
part of the modern province of Shantung; and it seems to
be the fact that all the specimens that have come to light
have been dug up in Shantung, except a few of the
so-called "Ming knives," which were found in the neigh-
bouring province of Chihli. Of the "large knives of
Ts'i" especially, the Ku Ch'üan Hui says that they have
all been excavated from Ts'i territory, and adds, what is
noteworthy, that they belong undoubtedly to the system
of T'ai Kung's Nine Treasuries. This proves that that
system in the view of some of the native critics could not
have been restricted to the issue of round money exclusively. The same work observes that "it has never
been contested that the knife money dates from the Chou
and Contending States' epochs"—say from B.C. 1120 to
B.C. 250.

The Chin Shih So, referring to the specimens which in
the "Catalogue" are Nos. 44 and 1029, considers they must
date from an earlier period than the other knives, and,
recalling the old legend contained in the Lu Shih, that
"Huang Ti fashioned metal knives and instituted the Five
kinds of treasure, pi," remarks that assuredly knives did
not make their first appearance in the State of Ts'i.

But if knives were used as money in any other region
than Shantung and Chihli, and specially the former, there
seems to remain no record of the fact.

M. Lacouperie on p. xi. of the Introduction, under the
years B.C. 679–675, informs us that "The State of Ts'i
being at war during these years, Prince Hwan was finally
afraid that his armoured bannermen were not sufficient in
number: in order to facilitate enlistment he successfully
authorized the payments of mulcts for slight offences with

their own metal knives, instead of the legal Ring currency, as heretofore since 950."

On p. 213 of the "Catalogue" we also find the following passage :—

"The introduction of the Knife money in the state of Ts'i, conterminous with the above [Shantung] peninsula, is attributed in a rather legendary way to the following circumstances, circa 650 B.C. At the eve of an expedition, the soldiers of the Duke Hwan, of Ts'i, proved dissatisfied with the stringent regulations on weights and money which had previously been enacted by the Prime Minister Kwan-Tze (see pp. 4, 18, and Introduction). Their General, afraid of their being disloyal, granted to them the authorization of making use of their metal knives for barter. The people were delighted with the innovation, which was giving them a more convenient medium of exchange, and adopted it eagerly. Hwai-nan tze, who died in 122 B.C., and to whom we are indebted for the preceding story, says that in his time they were still faithful to the practice, and, despite the changes and modifications which had happened in the currency, they continued to cast knife money similar to the patterns of former times."

I cannot account for this episode being attributed by M. Lacouperie to Huai Nan Tzŭ. As the extract from the latter author which follows, does not agree with M. Lacouperie's summarized narrative, and as no closer reference than to the Chinese author at large is given, I had the whole of his works searched through by a native scholar, with the result that no such story could be found, the only passage bearing upon the subject at all, apparently, being this :—

齊 桓 公 將 欲 征 伐 甲 兵 不 足 令 有 重 罪 者 出
犀 甲 一 戟 有 輕 罪 者 贖 以 金 分 訟 而 不 勝 者
出 一 束 煎 百 姓 皆 說 乃 矯 箭 爲 矢 鑄 金 而 爲 刃

"Huan, Duke of Ts'i, wished to go to war, but his arms and accoutrements being insufficient, he commanded that for the graver crimes the offender should pay a cuirass of rhinoceros hide and a three-pointed spear; for the lighter crimes the culprit should redeem himself with a portion of metal [or perhaps gold]; while unsuccessful litigants should pay a sheaf of arrows. The people were pleased at this, and made arrows out of the *chien*-bamboo and cast metal into blades, 刐."

It must be this passage which we find thus summarized in the Ku Ch'üan Hui (Section *Hsiang*, ch. 2, p. 1), but with an important variation:—

"Huai Nan Tzŭ says that Duke Huan, fearing his arms were insufficient, commanded that for lighter crimes the culprit should redeem himself with a metal knife. Duke Huan thus became rich and powerful. Throughout the history of the State of Ts'i, this was the traditional and unchanged coinage. As the natural result, specimens have been numerous up to the present day."

It will be seen that the characters 金 分, *chin fên*, of Huai Nan Tzŭ (I consulted the edition of Kao Yu, 高 誘), have become 金 刀, *chin tao*, in the Ku Ch'üan Hui. The variation in the two characters is easy to account for— omit the upper part of *fên* and there remains *tao*. *But which is right?* For unless the text of Huai Nan Tzŭ used both by the authors of the Ku Ch'üan Hui and of the Chin Shih So is the authentic one, this version of the origin of the knife money must be abandoned.

But I am fortunate enough to have discovered, as I believe, the source whence Huai Nan Tzŭ derived his information. That source is again Kuan Tzŭ, in whose eighth chapter, on the first page, occur these words:—

公 曰 民 辦 軍 事 矣 則 可 乎 對 曰 不 可 甲 兵 未
足 也 請 薄 刑 罰 以 厚 甲 兵 於 是 死 罪 不 殺 刑
罪 不 罰 使 以 甲 兵 贖 死 罪 以 犀 甲 一 戟 刑 罪
以 脅 盾 一 戟 過 罪 以 金 軍 無 所 計 而 訟 者 成
以 束 矢

"The Duke said, 'Now that the people understand the business of campaigning, is it feasible?' 'No,' was the answer, 'arms and accoutrements are insufficient. I would beg that you lighten the punishments, and thus add to your arms.' Thereupon death was no more inflicted for capital offences, nor their [respective] penalties for those of which maiming was the punishment, but the guilty were made to redeem themselves by the payment of arms and accoutrements. For capital offences a rhinoceros skin cuirass and one three-pointed spear; for offences punishable by maiming, a shield and three-pointed spear; for offences committed by misadventure, fines of metal [or perhaps gold] were inflicted. Where a charge was brought not included in the military code [so the commentator understands the words *chün wu so chi*], it was settled by the payment of a sheaf of arrows."

If this passage be authentic, it seems clearly to be the basis of Huai Nan Tzŭ's version. The "offences committed by misadventure" answer to the "lighter offences" of the later author, and the single word "metal," or perhaps "gold," of Kuan Tzŭ becomes in Huai Nan Tzŭ "a portion of metal" (or of gold), which does not sensibly modify the meaning, and, if I may indulge in a little conjecture, a trifling accommodation of the latter text, a mere deletion of two insignificant strokes, so as to transform 分 into 刀, or "portion" into "knife," on the part, perhaps, of some one with a theory, and we have the origin of this story of how knife money came into existence in the State of Ts'i.

But another and more formidable difficulty in accepting the story is furnished by the knife-coins themselves. In no sense could they have been used as weapons. Even the biggest of them, the "large knives of Ts'i" are only large as compared with the feeble little objects known as "knives of Chü" or "Ming knives." What sort of a weapon is a thin bronze blade not longer than a razor, but which, unlike a razor, is constructed with an "edge" made by a raised rim or lip as if specially provided to prevent its cutting? Yet such is the make of one of these terrible weapons now lying before me. Whatever may be the real origin of knife-coins, those that have come down to us are certainly not specimens of Duke Huan's ingeniously collected magazine of arms and accoutrements.

Ts'u tao, or *Chin ts'u tao,* 錯 刀 or 金 錯 刀. Inlaid knife, or Gold-inlaid knife.

Another form of knife-coin, very similar to the *ch'i tao,* was introduced by Wang Mang, and is so named because, as Vissering says, "the characters engraved on these coins, denoting the name and value, were washed with gold."

Ya shêng ch'ien, 壓 勝 錢. Coins of Domination.

This phrase is found written with 厭 for the first word, but in either case the reading is *ya* and not *yen.* The meaning of the name is Money possessing magic powers of dominating or subjugating (*ya shêng*) evil influences.

The term is said in the Po Ku T'u to have been introduced by Li Hsiao-mei, one of the earlier writers on numismatics, and is applied to various descriptions of medals and other pieces, used as charms—not true coins— of which figures will be found in the coin-books. The subjoined translation of a passage from a work entitled the Ch'i Shêng Chi, or Record of the Seven Holy Ones, is quoted in ch. 43 of the Ku Yü T'u Pu, and shows the functions of these Coins of Domination.

"The Supreme Ruler of the Tao [? Lao Tzŭ; 太上.道君 in the text] on the 15th day of the seventh moon ascended to the Lin Hall of the Nine Heavens, where he expounded the Law to the multitude of Devas, and thus addressed them: 'In the Earth below, the people are much afflicted with floods, drought, and pestilence.' Then was the Honoured Ruler of the Exquisite Dawn charged to convey a precious casket in which were placed two miracle-working Dragon Coins of Domination, to be left to guard the famous mountains and great rivers, and to remove disastrous influences."

Presumably these magic medals are of Taoist origin, but they are of little real importance to our subject. M. Lacouperie rightly remarks on p. xxxi. of the Introduction,

that " they have no regular connection with the currency,"
but disfigures a note on the same page by a grotesque
misrendering of the term as "*yen* [sic] *shing tsien*, 厭 勝 錢,
hardly-adequate-to-coins " !

Yü chia ch'ien, or *Chia ch'ien*, 榆 莢 錢, or 莢 錢. Elm
seed-vessel money.

Diminutive specimens of *cash* were cast in large quantities
in the early years of the Han dynasty, to which the above
terms were applied, and fittingly applied, considering the
size, shape, and tenuity of the well-known seed-vessel of
the elm tree. It is matter for surprise that with the word
莢, *chia*, a *pod* or *seed-vessel*, staring him in the face,
Vissering should have gone out of his way to mistranslate
the word as "elm-leaf," as he does on p. 29, thereby
converting a distinctly apt comparison into a quite
inappropriate one. But that M. Lacouperie should have
blindly followed him into this blunder is stranger still.

Yüan, 員. A round object, specially a round coin.

Modern usage restricts this, as a numerative, to officials,
curiously enough, while for foreign coins 圓 and 元 (both
pronounced *yüan*) are written.

The Shuo Wên tersely defines the word as the " numerative of objects." But the author of the Liu Shu Ku is
more communicative, and writes as follows: " Meaning:
Money (錢). T'ai Kung first cast metal into circles, 員,
to serve as a medium of exchange. They were round
externally and square internally, hence the character
consists of 口 [*wei*, of which the ancient shape was a
circle] and 貝 [*pei*, a *shell*]. They are now called *ch'ien*
or *cash*. The numerative of shells is 朋, *p'êng*, of coins,
員, *yüan*."

The Shuo Wên and the Liu Shu Ku do not, we may
note in passing, analyse the character in the same way.
According to the former, *wei*, the upper part, is merely
phonetic. In the preferable view of the Liu Shu Ku, the
character is an example of *hui i*, " suggestive compounds,"
in which the general idea of value indicated by 貝 is
combined with the special distinction of circularity, 口, to

suggest the word, and make up the character, 員, *yüan,* a *round coin.*

It should also be noticed that in the Liu Shu Ku the term *yüan fa* is always written 員 法, and not, as ordinarily, 圜 法·

The *yüan,* it will thus be seen, are what we now call *cash,* and so the same with the *yüan fa* of T'ai Kung. We are not warranted, I think, in identifying either the thing or the word with 鍰, *huan,* a metal ring, as M. Lacouperie has done on p. xvii.

The character itself is actually found on the coins inscribed *pan yüan,* 半 員, figured on pp. 320, 321 of the "Catalogue," and attributed by the author of the Ku Ch'üan Hui to the epoch of the Contending States.

Li Tso-hsien, in his notes on these coins, explains that 圜 is interchangeable with 圓, while the latter was anciently written 員, so that these three characters are convertible, and he interprets the inscription as meaning that the coin was equal in value to half a *yüan fa.*

Yüan fa, 圜 法. Currency, coinage, especially, perhaps exclusively, the coinage or coins of copper *cash.*

This term has been a stumbling-block to Vissering and M. Lacouperie. The former, p. 17, says that the term means "Round or current Rule." The latter, p. xix. of the Introduction, writes, " *Yuan-fah,* current rule, or better, rules of currency." Both have misconceived the force of the syllable *fa.* This does not here have reference to *law* or *rule,* but illustrates a very common usage of the word, namely *method, system.* In the modern colloquial language, to quote from Mateer's excellent " *Mandarin Lessons,*" p. 282, " 法 is much used as an affix to verbs, to denote the manner of the action. It is sometimes also joined to nouns, which it practically turns into verbs; thus 兵 法 means *drill,* but must be analysed as *the method of drilling soldiers, or of soldiering.* In all cases 法 is without accent . . ."

Thus, at the present day, 錢 法, *ch'ien fa,* is the ordinary term for the copper coinage, the currency, and means

literally the coin-system or coin-method. So 鈔 法 occurs
for the Chinese paper currency or note-system. And in
the same way, precisely, the old term *yüan fa* was used.
According as we consider *yüan* to mean "round" with
some, or with Yen Shih-ku to signify "uniform and
current" (均 而 通)—according, in fact, as we translate
it "circular" or "circulating"—the full term will mean
the system or method of round coins (*yüan*); or the system
of circulating currency: introduced, in either case, as
tradition constantly declared, by T'ai Kung when Minister
to the sovereign of Chou. By a natural transition the
coins themselves came to be spoken of by the same name,
yüan fa thus becoming synonymous with *ch'ien*. In numismatic works *yüan fa* is used to distinguish the round *cash*
from the knife- or *pu*-coins.

If the first analysis of the term be chosen, a word 圜,
yüan, meaning a *round coin*, is logically implied. With
that special meaning and in that special written form, I
have not met it, though the character constantly occurs
in the Shuo Wên's text, meaning *round, circular*, in general.
But as shown under the previous entry, we have a *pan
yüan* coin, while the Liu Shu Ku expressly affirms that
the synonymous character 貟 means *money, ch'ien*, and that
T'ai Kung first cast money in the form of circles, 一 貟,
yüan. Elsewhere the same work quotes a remark that when
ch'ien came into use as the word for money, the earlier
names *ch'üan* and *yüan*, 貟, became obsolete.

We do seem, therefore, to find traces of such a word
as we are in quest of, and Tai T'ung in writing 貟 法
for the term *yüan fa* is perhaps historically justified.

Yüan pao, 元 寶. (1) A name first applied to *cash* in
the opening reign of the T'ang dynasty. (2) A "shoe"
of sycee or silver bullion.

It does not seem certain which of these senses is the
earlier, nor, supposing it to be the second, what the true
significance of the name is. We might, perhaps, conjecture
the meaning to be silver of "prime (元, *yüan*) value,"
i.e. of the highest purity, A writer named Wêng Shu-p'ei,

the author of a book on coins, and evidently much esteemed by his fellow-author of the Ku Ch'üan Hui, is quoted in the latter work (Section *Shou Chi*, ch. 4) on this point. He says:—

"The words *t'ung pao* (通 寶), or 'current valuable,' on coins derive their meaning from the currency (流 通) of the latter. But in the term *yüan pao* the word *yüan* has no derivation. It is nothing but a traditional phrase dating from the *K'ai t'ung* money [viz. the *cash* cast about A.D. 622, in the 4th year of Wu Tê]. At that time *yüan pao* was a name for a wealthy man. Under the Yüan dynasty, in the reign Chung T'ung, *yüan pao* was a term for a banknote, and subsequently the same expression was applied to silver ingots."

Wêng's opinion evidently was that there first existed a phrase associated with wealth, but the origin of which is obscure, and that under the circumstances, to be immediately explained, this phrase became, by a popular error, a name for the new copper *cash*, later for banknotes also, and lastly for silver bullion.

The origin of the term as applied to *cash* is curious. I do not know if it has been given before, but Vissering, who devotes some three pages to the *K'ai yüan cash* (pp. 100–102), does not allude to it.

It is thus narrated in the History of the Earlier T'ang dynasty, as cited in the Chin Shih So. After stating that in the fourth year of the Wu Tê period, A.D. 622, the 5-*shu* currency of the preceding Sui dynasty was abandoned, and a new type of coins introduced, bearing the legend *K'ai yüan t'ung pao*, 開 元 通 寶, or "current money of the inauguration," various details are added, and the passage goes on—"The inscription commenced at the top, continued at the bottom, was resumed at the left hand, and ended on the right.[1] If the legend were read round the coin,

---

[1] As Vissering correctly points out, p. 102, note 2, the usage of these terms with respect to coins is exactly the reverse of ours, though it conforms to European heraldic practice. The "left" of a coin, as Chinese call it, is our "right." However, the practice must have varied, for "right" and "left" in the Ku Ch'üan Hui are the same as with us. Is this an archaism?

beginning at the top and going on to the left [our *right*], it also made sense, and so the common custom was to speak of *K'ai t'ung yüan pao* money." The same authority relates that for a short time in the subsequent reign of Ch'ien Fêng, A.D. 666–668, the legend was actually inscribed in conformity with the prevailing popular practice, but almost immediately reverted to the standard disposition of the characters, which usually obtained afterwards.

Although the adoption of *yüan pao* as a numismatic term was thus due to a popular freak, we are justified in supposing that the expression already existed, and most likely as the Ku Ch'üan Hui asserts, with such a sense that its association with coins would not seem inappropriate. The words *k'ai t'ung* are still used to denote the idea of *opening, commencing, initiating*.

The point is not strictly germane to the early history of money, but it may not be altogether out of place, in connection with this term, to notice the singular errors into which M. Lacouperie has fallen in the following passage on p. xxv. of the Introduction :—

" *Sycee,* Chinese 細 絲, fine silk, is the general term for lump silver, and is explained as meaning that, if pure, it may be drawn out under the application of heat into *fine silk-like* threads. This is, of course, a script-etymology, and pure fancy, derived from the ideographical meaning inherent in the symbols, while the historical etymology must be sought for in a foreign term transliterated thereby. *Yuen-pao,* 元 寶, is the common name among foreigners for the silver ingot which bears some resemblance to a native shoe."

Thus M. Lacouperie. Now for some facts. The statement as to *sycee* M. Lacouperie cites from Mr. Giles' "Glossary of Reference," and, as we have seen, he takes exception to the explanation of the term there given. That explanation, though usual, is not, I believe, in fact the correct one, as the subjoined translation of a note on the subject by a Chinese formerly in the Banking business shows, while it also disposes of M. Lacouperie's supposed " foreign term transliterated " by the characters.

"細 絲 紋 銀 [literally, Fine silk line silver]. The term *sycee* (fine silk) originated in the Five Northern Provinces [Chihli, Shantung, Shansi, Shensi, and Honan]. When the Shansi Bankers melt silver into ingots, after it has been liquefied and poured into the mould, and before it has again solidified, the mould is lightly tapped, when there appear on the surface of the silver fine, silk-like, circular lines. The higher the 'touch' of the metal, the more like fine silk are these 'circlings' on the surface of the silver. Hence ingots of full quality are classified as *sycee*."

It merely remains to add that the pronunciation of the two characters as '*sycee*,' represents the Cantonese and *not* the northern sounds, due, no doubt, to the fact that the Europeans who first introduced this word heard it from the lips of their Cantonese Compradores, who adopted it from the Shansi Bankers—for it does not appear to be a Cantonese phrase at all — giving the characters their Cantonese values.

I was much mystified by M. Lacouperie's perversely incorrect statement that " *Yüen pao* is the common name among foreigners for the silver ingot which bears some resemblance to the native shoe," when any resident of six months' standing in China could have informed him that the term *yüan pao* is never used by foreigners. The explanation is simple. M. Lacouperie has taken this sentence from Mr. Giles' " *Glossary of Reference*," p. 128, omitting the initial words " Shoes (of Silver): 元 寶." It is, of course, the " shoe" which is "the common term among foreigners," and not *yüan pao*.

[It should be noted that this article was received some time before the lamented death of Mr. Lacouperie. The writer, having in the meantime returned to China, could not easily be consulted as to any alterations he would, under the circumstances, have wished to make in it; so it has been thought best to print the article without material change.—ED.]

www.ingramcontent.com/pod-product-compliance
Lightning Source LLC
Chambersburg PA
CBHW021525090426
42739CB00007B/784